Practice Book

CENTER STAGE

Express Yourself in English

3

D1599574

Lynn Bonesteel
Samuela Eckstut-Didier

Series Consultants
MaryAnn Florez   Sharon Seymour

PEARSON
Longman

Center Stage 3: Express Yourself in English
Practice Book

Pearson Education, 10 Bank Street, White Plains, NY 10606

Staff credits: The people who made up the **Center Stage 3 Practice Book** team,
representing editorial, production, design, and manufacturing are
Pietro Alongi, Wendy Campbell, Diane Cipollone, Dave Dickey,
Warren Fischbach, Aliza Greenblatt, Ray Keating, and Melissa Leyva.

Text composition: ElectraGraphics, Inc.

Text font: 9.5/11 Minion Pro

Photo credits: p. 3 Royalty-free/Corbis; **p. 33** (first) Kevin Peterson/AgeFotoStock, (second) Glow Images/AgeFotoStock;
p. 44 Royalty-free/Corbis; **p. 62** Mitch Hrdlicka/Getty Images; **p. 67** Peter Scholey/Getty Images;
p. 88 John Liend/Tiffany Schoepp/Getty Images

Illustration credits: A Corazón Abierto (Marcela Gómez), Steve Attoe, Laurie Conley,
Debby Fisher, Marty Harris, Christopher Hitz, Francisco Morales, Mari Rodríguez,
Steve Schulman, Wendy Smith, Gary Torrisi, Meryl Treatner, Ralph Voltz

ISBN-13: 978-0-13-607018-4
ISBN-10: 0-13-607018-3

Pearsonlongman on the Web
Pearsonlongman.com offers online resources for teachers and students.
Access our Companion Websites, our online catalog, and our local offices around the world.
Visit us at **pearsonlongman.com.**

Printed in the United States of America
1 2 3 4 5 6 7 8 9 10—BR—12 11 10 09 08

Contents

UNIT 1 VOCABULARY EXERCISES

 A Look at the picture. Complete the sentences. Use the words in the box.

~~bangs~~	curly hair	straight hair
a beard	mustaches	wavy hair

1. Ron and Felicia haven't got _____bangs_____.

2. Betsy and Marco have got _____.

3. Ron and Lupe have got _____.

4. Felicia has got _____.

5. Marco and Chris have got _____.

6. Only Chris has got _____.

B   **Complete the conversation. Use the words in the box.**

am getting to know	a bad temper	a nice personality
am going out with	get along with	sense of humor

Maria: Mark is my new neighbor. I ___am getting to know___ him.
                                                    1.

Isabel: Really? I _____ Mark. He's my boyfriend.
                                    2.

Maria: Wow! That's great. He's got _____. I like him.
                                                        3.

Isabel: Yeah. He makes me laugh, too. I like his _____.
                                                                    4.

Maria: Do you _____ his brother Ben?
                                5.

Isabel: No, I don't. He has _____. He's always angry.
                                            6.

UNIT 1 GRAMMAR EXERCISES

Grammar to Communicate 1:
Have got: Statements

A Complete the sentences with true information about you and your English teacher. Use *'ve got, 's got, haven't got,* or *hasn't got.*

1. I ___*'ve got* OR *haven't got*___ brown eyes.

2. I _____ blue eyes.

3. I _____ straight hair.

4. I _____ curly hair.

5. My teacher _____ glasses.

6. My teacher _____ long hair.

7. My teacher _____ bangs.

8. My teacher _____ gray hair.

B Look at the photo of Carolina Coelho. Then complete each sentence. Circle the letter of the correct answer.

1. Carolina _____ from Brazil.

    a. has got   **b.** is

2. Carolina _____ short.

    a. hasn't got   **b.** isn't

3. _____ average height.

    a. She's got   **b.** She's

4. She _____ a teacher.

    a. has   **b.** is

5. Carolina and Marco _____ an 8-year-old son, Paul.

    a. have got   **b.** has got

6. _____ got a cat named Fluffy.

    a. They've   **b.** They're

Grammar to Communicate 2:
Present Progressive: Extended Time

A Complete the conversations. Write short answers.

1. **A:** Are you working these days?

   B: _____ Yes, I am _____. I started a new job about a month ago.

2. **A:** Are you taking any classes this semester?

   B: _____. I haven't got time to study.

3. **A:** Is your mother visiting again?

   B: _____. She's staying with us for a week.

4. **A:** Is your son going to school?

   B: _____. He's only four. He's too young.

5. **A:** Are your daughter and son-in-law living with you?

   B: _____, but they're looking for an apartment.

6. **A:** Are you making a lot of money?

   B: _____, but I love my job.

B Complete the e-mail message. Use the present progressive.

Dear Annie,

Thanks for your message. I _'m doing_____ much better these days.
                          1. (do)
I _____ a lot of new people, and guess what? Betsy Parker and
   2. (meet)
I _____ out! We _____ along great. But there's
   3. (go)   **4. (get)**
one problem. I _____ much time on my classes, and the work
              5. (not spend)
_____ more and more difficult. Betsy _____ any
6. (get)   **7. (not, have)**
problems with her classes. But that's no surprise—she _____
                                                      8. (study)
right now, and I'm not! Anyway, write again soon.

Take care,

Kerry

NAME: _____   DATE: _____

Grammar to Communicate 3:
Simple Present and Present Progressive

A   **Complete the paragraph. Circle the correct answer. Write it on the line.**

My daughter always _____ *does* _____ very well at school,
             1. (does / is doing)

but this year she _____ a hard time. I think it's
             2. (has / is having)

because she and her best friend _____ these days.
             3. (don't get along / aren't getting along)

And my daughter is shy, so she _____ a lot of other
             4. (doesn't have / isn't having)

friends. She usually _____ school, but this year she
             5. (loves / is loving)

_____ well at all.
      6. (doesn't do / isn't doing)

B   **Complete the conversations. Use the simple present or the present progressive.**

1. **A:** What _____ *is going* _____ on with Stan these days? He's so quiet!
          (go)

     B: Maybe his restaurant _____ well.
            (not do)

2. **A:** Where is Mrs. Johnson this summer? _____ her
               (she / visit)

     grandchildren again?

     B: Of course. She always _____ the summer with
            (spend)

     them.

3. **A:** You're really lucky that you _____ along with your
            (get)

     boss.

     B: Yeah, he _____ a great personality.
           (have)

4. **A:** _____ a lot of parties this summer?
        (your neighbors / have)

     B: Oh yes. It's the same every summer. They _____
              (have)

     people over every weekend.

Review and Challenge

Find the mistake in each conversation. Circle the letter and correct the mistake.

1. **A:** <u>Are</u> you <u>have</u> a dog?
       (A)   B

    Correct: _____*Do*_____

    B: No, I <u>don't</u>, but <u>I've got</u> two cats and a fish.
           C   D

2. **A:** How <u>is</u> your son <u>doing</u> at college?
           A   B

    Correct: _____

    B: Fine. <u>He's study</u> really hard.
          C D

3. **A:** <u>Does</u> your teacher <u>have</u> a nice personality?
        A   B

    Correct: _____

    B: Yes, and she <u>is</u> <u>got</u> a great sense of humor.
               C D

4. **A:** What <u>is</u> your new boss <u>like</u>?
            A   B

    Correct: _____

    B: <u>She's</u> not very nice. She's <u>get</u> a bad temper.
        C   D

5. **A:** What <u>does</u> your boyfriend <u>look like</u>?
           A   B

    Correct: _____

    B: He <u>has got</u> tall, and he <u>has</u> beautiful brown eyes.
        C   D

6. **A:** <u>Do</u> you <u>know</u> your new neighbors?
       A   B

    Correct: _____

    B: No, but we <u>get</u> <u>to know</u> them.
           C   D

7. **A:** <u>Are</u> Tom and Joyce <u>going</u> out these days?
       A   B

    Correct: _____

    B: No, they <u>don't</u>, but <u>they're</u> still good friends.
           C   D

8. **A:** Why <u>you're</u> <u>wearing</u> jeans?
         A   B

    Correct: _____

    B: Because <u>I've</u> got the day off. <u>It's</u> a holiday.
          C   D

9. **A:** Where <u>are</u> <u>your parents</u> <u>staying</u>?
          A   B   C

    Correct: _____

    B: They <u>stay</u> at a hotel.
          D

10. **A:** <u>Do you</u> <u>have</u> a pencil?
        A   B

    Correct: _____

    B: I <u>haven't got</u> a pencil, but <u>I got</u> a pen.
        C   D

UNIT 2 VOCABULARY EXERCISES

A   Complete the conversation. Use the words in the box.

a farm	public transportation	a tourist
a parking space	~~skyscraper~~	traffic

Hyeon Jung: Excuse me. What's the name of that tall building?

Kim: It's called the Lake Point Tower. It's my favorite _____skyscraper_____
1.
in Chicago. Are you _____?
2.

Hyeon Jung: Yes. I'm visiting for the weekend. I live on _____ in
3.
the country.

Kim: Do you like Chicago?

Hyeon Jung: I love it. But there's too much _____! In my country,
4.
we don't have a lot of cars.

Kim: Yeah. It's also difficult to find _____ for your car.
5.

Hyeon Jung: Do you take _____?
6.

Kim: Yes. I take it every day.

Hyeon Jung: Oh, good. How do I get to the State Street station?

B   Complete the sentences. Use the words in the box. Use capital letters as needed.

~~crime~~	a field	pollution
a factory	parking	sunshine

1.   My neighborhood is very dangerous. There's a lot of _____crime_____.

2.   Anna works in _____. She makes cars.

3.   _____ is a place where you can see cows.

4.   There's too much _____. I can't see the sky.

5.   Please walk to my party. There isn't enough _____ for all the cars.

6.   Andre likes to go to the beach and enjoy the _____.

UNIT 2 GRAMMAR EXERCISES

Grammar to Communicate 1:
Count and Noncount Nouns: Quantifiers

A   **Complete each conversation. Circle the correct answer.**

1. **A:** There isn't much crime these days.

   B: Yes. **It's a big problem.** / (We're lucky.)

2. **A:** There are many tourists.

   B: I know. There **are / aren't** a lot of places to visit.

3. **A:** There are a few skyscrapers here.

   B: Yes. This is a **village / small city.**

4. **A:** There aren't many cars.

   B: That's because **many / few** people drive.

5. **A:** There is very little traffic.

   B: Yes. There's **a lot of / very little** air pollution.

B **Rewrite the sentences. Keep a similar meaning. Make the nouns plural if necessary.**

1. There isn't much sunshine.   _There aren't many sunny days._
                                          (sunny day)

2. There aren't many parking spaces. _____
                                          (parking)

3. There's some parking out back.   _____
                                          (parking space)

4. There aren't any buses or trains. _____
                                          (public transportation)

5. There's very little open space.   _____
                                          (field)

6. There are very few cars.   _____
                                          (traffic)

7. There is a lot of crime.   _____
                                          (criminal)

8. There is no work.   _____
                                          (job)

NAME: _____   DATE: _____

Grammar to Communicate 2:
Count and Noncount Nouns: *Plenty of / Enough / Too much / Too many*

A   **Match the sentences. Write the correct letters.**

  _d_ **1.** There's too much rain.   **a.** I don't like tall buildings.

  ____ **2.** There are too many tourists.   **b.** They make too much noise.

  ____ **3.** There are too many skyscrapers. **c.** It's not very safe.

  ____ **4.** There aren't enough cabs.   **d.** We need ~~more sunshine~~.

  ____ **5.** There are plenty of parks here.   **e.** Yes, it's "The Green City."

  ____ **6.** There's too much crime.   **f.** It's impossible to find one when it rains.

B   **Complete the conversations. Write affirmative or negative sentences. Use *There is / are* and *too many, too much, not enough,* or *plenty of*.**

1. A: ___There aren't enough___ hotels for all of the tourists.

    B: I know. They need to build more.

2. A: _____ parking downtown.

    B: I agree! I can never find a space.

3. A: _____ cars, but not enough highways.

    B: Yes. The traffic is terrible.

4. A: _____ pollution in this city.

    B: You're right. It's because there are too many cars.

5. A: The weather's great today.

    B: Yes, it is. _____ sunshine.

6. A: _____ good restaurants.

    B: I know. There are only fast food places.

Grammar to Communicate 3:
Both / Neither / Either

A   Write a ✓ if the sentence is correct. Write an ✗ if it is incorrect. Then correct the incorrect sentences.

   _✗_ 1. Both ~~of~~ neighborhoods have plenty of kids.

   _✓_ 2. Neither neighborhood has many trees.

   _____ 3. We would like to live in either of the neighborhoods.

   _____ 4. Both of the neighborhoods is friendly.

   _____ 5. There isn't much parking in neither neighborhood.

   _____ 6. But parking is not a problem because either of us has a car.

   _____ 7. There are several apartments available in both of the neighborhoods.

   _____ 8. Both of the neighborhoods aren't large.

B   Rewrite the sentences. Use the words in parentheses. Keep the same meaning.

1. Both places are small.

   _____Neither place is_____ big.
          (neither)

2. Neither apartment is in a good location.

   _____ in bad locations.
         (both)

3. We dislike both of the apartments.

   We don't like _____.
              (either)

4. Neither of the apartments is cheap.

   _____ expensive.
         (both)

5. The lobby is not clean in either building.

   The lobby is dirty _____.
              (both)

6. Both of the buildings are dark.

   _____ sunny.
         (neither)

7. We like neither of the landlords.

   We don't like _____.
            (either)

Review and Challenge

Correct the e-mail. There are eight mistakes. The first mistake is corrected for you.

Dear Julia,

How are you? I think about you several times a day, but I never seem to have
enough
~~too much~~ time to write. Anyway, I have very few minutes now, and I have a lot

news!

The new apartment is great. There are several window in every room, so

there's plenty light. Actually, there's too much light right now—I have no

curtains, and no time to buy any. The apartment's also very quiet. There are

only three apartments in this building, and neither of my neighbors is home

very much. There's only a little traffic on the street during the day and any

traffic at night.

What else? My neighbors seem friendly. Both them are college students too.

When I have a little free time, I'm going to invite them over for coffee. I'm

really busy, but I'm lonely too. Anyway, I have many homework, so I'll say

good-bye for now. I'll write again soon.

Love,

Janet

UNIT 3 VOCABULARY EXERCISES

A   Complete the conversations. Use the words in the box.

court	goal	missed	pass	runs	~~team~~

1. **A:** What's your favorite _____team_____?
   B: I really like the Lions.

2. **A:** Was he disappointed?
   B: Yes, because he _____ the shot.

3. **A:** Who's winning the baseball game?
   B: The Sharks. They have five _____ and the Dolphins only have two.

4. **A:** Where do you play basketball?
   B: On a _____ near my house.

5. **A:** Did Ramon _____ the ball to Jim?
   B: Yes, and he made the shot!

6. **A:** Ben scored a _____ in the soccer game.
   B: That's great!

B   Complete the sports report. Use the words in the box.

~~beat~~	cheered	lost to	points	scored	was tied

Last night in baseball, the Jaguars _____beat_____ the Sharks.
1.
The Jaguar fans _____ for their best player, Mickey Halls.
2.
He had a great night. Also in baseball, the Tigers _____ the
3.
Bulldogs. The Tiger fans were disappointed. This was the third loss for the team.

In an exciting soccer game between the Royals and the Patriots, Tim
Yang _____ twice, and the Patriots won. In basketball
4.
news, the Browns played the Kings. Five minutes before the end, the score
_____. Both teams had 52 _____. But at
5.   6.
the last minute, the Browns won. Also in basketball . . . .

UNIT 3 GRAMMAR EXERCISES

Grammar to Communicate 1:
Simple Past: Regular and Irregular Verbs

A Complete the sentences. Use the past tense of the verbs in the box. (Be careful! Some sentences are affirmative, and some are negative.)

be	beat	~~lose~~	pass	play	score	~~watch~~	win

1. I ___didn't watch___ the game on TV. I listened to it on the radio.

2. It was a terrible game. My team ____lost____.

3. The best player _____ any goals. He missed every time.

4. The fans _____ happy. They didn't cheer.

5. We _____ that team last year, but this year we lost to them.

6. The players on the other team _____ the ball to each other nicely.

7. They _____ because they played very well.

8. We lost because our team _____ well.

B Rewrite the sentences. Keep the same meaning. (Be careful! Some sentences are affirmative, and some are negative.)

1. Our team didn't win.   ___Our team lost.___
                                        (lose)

2. We lost to the best team.   _____
                                        (beat)

3. We were nervous before the game. _____
                                        (be relaxed)

4. The game didn't start on time. _____
                                        (start late)

5. Our best player was hurt.   _____
                                        (be in good shape)

6. We didn't expect to win.   _____
                                        (expect to lose)

7. But we felt bad after the game. _____
                                        (feel good)

Grammar to Communicate 2:
Simple Past: Questions

A Complete each conversation. Write a short and a long answer.

1. **Julie:** Was it a long game?

   Jen: No, __it wasn't__ . _____It was short_____ .

   (be / short)

2. **Julie:** Did you win?

   Jen: Yes, __we did__ . _____We beat them_____ .

   (beat / them)

3. **Julie:** Was it a close game?

   Jen: Yes, _____ . _____ .

   (almost / win)

4. **Julie:** Did you score any points?

   Jen: Yes, _____ . _____ .

   (score / ten points)

5. **Julie:** Congratulations! Did you go out after the game?

   Jen: No, _____ . _____ .

   (go / home)

B Write information questions about last year's team.

1. How many games did your team win last year?
   (how many games / your team / win / last year)

2. Who scored the most runs?
   (who / score / the most runs)

3. _____
   (who / be / the best player on the team)

4. _____
   (how many / players / be / on the team)

5. _____
   (where / you / play / most of your games)

6. _____
   (why / you / miss /so many games)

7. _____
   (what / happen / at the last game)

8. _____
   (who / the manager / hire / to be the new coach)

Grammar to Communicate 3:
Clauses with *Because, Before, After, As soon as*

A   **Complete each sentence. Circle the letter of the correct answer.**

1. Because the Stars' best player was hurt, _____
   - **a.** they didn't expect to win.
   - **b.** their fans were very happy.

2. As soon as they came out on the field, _____
   - **a.** everybody cheered.
   - **b.** they lost.

3. Before the game started, _____
   - **a.** the players took showers.
   - **b.** the players looked nervous.

4. As soon as they started to play, _____
   - **a.** they weren't nervous anymore.
   - **b.** they lost.

5. Because they won, _____
   - **a.** their fans were excited.
   - **b.** their fans were upset.

6. They went out to celebrate after _____
   - **a.** they finished playing.
   - **b.** they lost the game.

B   **Combine the sentences. Use *after, before, as soon as*, or *because*. Use commas if necessary. (There may be more than one correct answer.)**

1. The coach didn't choose Ann. She wasn't very good.

   The coach didn't choose Ann because she wasn't very good.

   OR *Because Ann wasn't very good, the coach didn't choose her.*

2. The coach saw Jessica play. He invited her to join the team.

   _____

3. He wanted her on the team. She was an excellent player.

   _____

4. Jessica joined the team. The team didn't win very often.

   _____

5. Jessica started playing. The team started to win.

   _____

6. The team won the championship. Jessica was on the team.

   _____

7. They won the championship. They went out to celebrate.

   _____

Review and Challenge

Find the mistake in each conversation. Circle the letter and correct the mistake.

1. **A:** Guess what? I <u>saw</u> Michael Jordan
      A

   downtown <u>yesterday</u>!
                  B

   B: Really? <u>Did</u> you <u>got</u> his autograph?
                  C   (D)

   Correct: _____*get*_____

2. **A:** <u>You did hear</u> the news about Ben?
           A   B

   B: No, <u>I didn't</u>. Did he <u>quit</u> the Angels?
                C   D

   Correct: _____

3. **A:** <u>Why did</u> Tony Harris <u>leave</u> the game?
           A   B

   B: He <u>did leave</u> because he <u>hurt</u> his knee.
              C   D

   Correct: _____

4. **A:** <u>What</u> <u>the score was</u> in last night's game?
           A   B

   B: I <u>don't</u> know. I <u>went</u> to bed early.
              C   D

   Correct: _____

5. **A:** Where <u>were</u> you? I <u>didn't see</u> you.
                 A   B

   B: I <u>was</u> late, so I <u>not got</u> a seat.
              C   D

   Correct: _____

6. **A:** What <u>happened</u> to the Rangers?
                A

   B: <u>As soon</u> Raven <u>left</u>, they <u>started</u> to lose.
           B   C   D

   Correct: _____

7. **A:** <u>How old was</u> Pelé when he <u>started</u> playing soccer?
           A   B

   B: It was <u>before</u> he <u>did start</u> school.
                 C   D

   Correct: _____

8. **A:** <u>Who</u> <u>did win</u> the World Cup last year?
           A   B

   B: <u>Was it</u> Brazil? I only <u>watched</u> a few games.
           C   D

   Correct: _____

9. **A:** We <u>lost</u> because we <u>hadn't</u> our best player.
              A   B

   B: No, they <u>beat</u> you <u>because</u> they were better.
                    C   D

   Correct: _____

UNIT 4 VOCABULARY EXERCISES

A Complete the story. Use the words in the box.

burning	daydreaming	fell off the ladder
~~climbed a ladder~~	dropped	went down the stairs
cut	fell down the stairs	

Mike had a very bad day! He wanted to paint his house. He

_____climbed a ladder_____ and started at the top. While he was painting, he saw
1.

a bee. He is afraid of bees. He moved too fast and _____.
2.

He got up, but the bee was still near him. While he was running from the bee,

he _____ the paint can.
3.

Later, while Mike was making lunch, he was _____
4.

about Jennifer Lopez. He was chopping carrots and _____
5.

his hand. He went upstairs to the bathroom to clean his hand. But while he

was climbing the stairs, his shoe came off—it _____. Mike
6.

_____. At the bottom of the stairs he smelled something
7.

strange. He went to the kitchen. His carrots were _____!
8.

When he left the kitchen, he didn't turn off the stove.

B Write the correct word beneath the picture. Use the words in the box.

~~break~~	chop	iron	slip

1. ___break___   2. _____   3. _____   4. _____

UNIT 4 GRAMMAR EXERCISES

Grammar to Communicate 1:
Past Progressive: Statements

A **Match the beginnings of the sentences to their endings. Write the correct letters.**

_d_ 1. He fell off his bike, but he didn't get hurt because

____ 2. He was in a car accident, but

____ 3. It wasn't raining in the morning, so

____ 4. He got a ticket because

____ 5. He wasn't working because

____ 6. He wasn't paying attention, so

____ 7. His children weren't feeling well, so

a. he was speeding.

b. he didn't hear the teacher.

c. he stayed home with them.

d. ~~he was wearing a helmet.~~

e. he wasn't driving.

f. he didn't take his umbrella.

g. it was a holiday.

B **At 7:00 last night, there was a fire at the Bartletts' house. Complete the sentences about what the family members were doing. (Be careful! Some are affirmative, and some are negative.)**

1. Sammi Bartlett was at the park. He _____was playing_____ baseball.
   (play)

2. Grandpa Bartlett was at the park too, but he _____ baseball. He was watching the game.
   (play)

3. Grandma Bartlett and the baby _____. The fire alarm woke them up.
   (sleep)

4. Mr. Bartlett and Sue _____ the dog. They always take the dog for a walk at 7:00.
   (walk)

5. Sue's older sister Pam _____ with them. She was doing her homework.
   (walk)

6. Mrs. Bartlett was on the phone. She and her sister _____.
   (talk)

7. Mr. Bartlett was in his car. He _____. He
   (work)
   _____ home from work.
   (drive)

NAME: _____   DATE: _____

Grammar to Communicate 2:
Past Progressive: Questions

A   **Match the questions with the answers. Write the correct letters.**

_b_ **1.** Why were you out at 2:00 A.M.?

____ **2.** Were any other people out?

____ **3.** Where was the man standing?

____ **4.** What was he wearing?

____ **5.** Was he carrying anything?

____ **6.** What was he doing?

____ **7.** What was he saying?

a. I'm not sure. A long coat, I think.

b. ~~I was walking my dog.~~

c. No, just me and my dog.

d. Behind a tree.

e. Yes, he was. He had a large bag.

f. I don't know. He was talking fast.

g. He was talking on a cell phone.

B   **Billy Bradley was in a car accident. A police officer is asking him some questions. Write the questions. Use the past progressive.**

Police: _Where were you going at the time of the accident_?
　　　　　　　1. (where / you go / at the time of the accident)
Billy: We were going to the hospital. My mom was sick.

Police: _____?
　　　　　　　　　　2. (who / drive)
Billy: I was.

Police: _____? You're only 15!
　　　　　　　　　　3. (why / you /drive)
Billy: Because my mother was too sick to drive.

Police: _____?
　　　　　　　　　　4. (where / your mother/ sit)
Billy: In the backseat.

Police: _____?
　　　　　　　　　　5. (you and your mother / wear / seatbelts)
Billy: My mother was, but I wasn't.

Police: _____?
　　　　　　　　　　6. (how fast / you/ drive)
Billy: I don't know.

Police: _____?
　　　　　　　　　　7. (it / rain/ a lot)
Billy: Yes, it was. The roads were terrible.

Grammar to Communicate 3:
Past Progressive and Simple Past: *When* and *While*

A Complete each sentence. Circle the correct answer.

1. We were sleeping when you (called) / were calling.

2. While you were having fun, your father **worked / was working**.

3. He screamed when he **cut / was cutting** his finger.

4. I **didn't pay / wasn't paying** attention when the teacher called on me.

5. While they were sleeping, someone **took / was taking** their car.

6. I felt terrible when I **broke / was breaking** my mother's favorite dish.

7. It **rained / was raining** when I woke up this morning.

B Look at the pictures. Complete the sentences. Use the simple past or the past progressive of the verbs in the box. You may use the verbs more than once.

break	chop	cut	drop	go	slip
burn	climb	daydream	fall	iron	

1. He <u>was climbing</u> a ladder when he ____<u>fell</u>____ off.

2. While she _____ down the stairs, she _____ down.

3. The glass _____ when he _____ it.

4. He _____ his hand while he _____.

5. He _____ while he _____.

6. She _____ onions when she _____ her finger.

Review and Challenge

Correct the paragraph. There are ten mistakes. The first mistake is corrected for you.

     I had a terrible day last Friday. First, I didn't hear my alarm clock, so I
~~was getting~~ *got* up late. I didn't have time to take a shower or eat my breakfast. I just got
dressed and run out the door. While I were walking to the train station, it started
to rain. I didn't have an umbrella. I wasn't want to get wet, so I started to run. I
running when I slipped and dropped my books. While I pick them up, I heard the
train. I ran to the station, but it was too late. The train was leave when I got there.
When I finally got to class, all of the students leaving. Class was over! I walked back
to the train station in the rain. Then I go home and got back into bed. I didn't
waking up until the next morning.

UNIT 5 VOCABULARY EXERCISES

A   **Complete the sentences. Use the words in the box.**

change a diaper	feed	give . . . a bath
dress	~~gave birth~~	

1. Tilda _____gave birth_____ last night. The baby is a girl!

2. Mike knows how to _____, but he doesn't like the smell!

3. Noriko used to _____ her baby breakfast every morning.

4. Emily didn't use to _____ her daughter in pink clothes.

5. Sam used to _____ his son _____ every night. He loved it!

B   **Complete the story. Use the words in the box.**

get dressed up	repairs	wears casual clothes
~~make her own clothes~~	throw away	

Lucia's grandmother used to do many things differently than Lucia does today. Lucia's grandmother used to _make her own clothes_ . Lucia buys
                                                                                    1.
her clothes at the store. Her grandmother's clothes were different, too. Her
grandmother used to _____ for a date, but Lucia wears jeans
                              2.
and a T-shirt on a date. In fact, Lucia _____ most of the time.
                                                     3.
She never wears dresses. Lucia's grandmother was very careful with money. She
didn't use to _____ dresses. She made them into blankets.
                        4.
Lucia doesn't keep old dresses. What is the biggest difference between Lucia and
her grandmother? Lucia's grandmother didn't use to drive! But Lucia drives and
_____ her own car!
            5.

UNIT 5 GRAMMAR EXERCISES

Grammar to Communicate 1:
Used to: Statements

A   **Complete each sentence. Circle the correct answer.**

1. People didn't use to have washing machines, so they
   a. wash clothes by hand.   (b.) used to wash clothes by hand.

2. Families used to eat at home, but now
   a. they eat out a lot.   b. they don't eat out a lot.

3. People didn't use to buy vegetables because
   a. they used to go to the store.   b. they used to grow their own.

4. In the past, people used to have a lot of children, but now
   a. many people have only two.   b. they used to have only two.

5. Nowadays we buy bread at the supermarket, but in the past people
   a. make their own bread.   b. used to make their own bread.

6. On a date, the woman never used to pay for herself, but today
   a. she often does.   b. she used to.

7. Young people didn't use to go to the mall because
   a. there aren't any malls.   b. there didn't use to be any malls.

B   **Complete the sentences. Use *used to* or *didn't use to* and the words in the box.**

change diapers	~~feed~~	give birth	repair
~~dress~~	get dressed up	make their own clothes	

1. Babies need help with their clothes. Fathers ___*didn't use to dress*___ their
   babies, but now many do.

2. Only mothers ___*used to feed*___ their babies milk and formula, but
   now many fathers do too.

3. People _____ for work, but now many people wear
   casual clothes.

4. People _____ broken things, but now they throw them away.

5. Women _____ at a hospital, but now they usually do.

6. Women _____, but now they buy clothes at stores.

Grammar to Communicate 2:
Used to: *Yes* / *No* Questions

A Complete the conversations about children's lives 200 years ago. Use affirmative or negative short answers.

1. **A:** Did most children use to go to school?   **B:** No, _they didn't_ .

2. **A:** Did young children use to work?   **B:** Yes, _they did_ .

3. **A:** Did girls use to take care of younger children?   **B:** Yes, _____.

4. **A:** Did girls and boys use to do the same chores?   **B:** No, _____.

5. **A:** Did girls use to go out alone at night?   **B:** No, _____.

6. **A:** Did children use to have a lot of free time?   **B:** No, _____.

7. **A:** Did boys use to work with their fathers?   **B:** Yes, _____.

B Read the answers. Then write questions. Use *used to* and the words in the boxes.

children	people
men	women

cook every day	go to bed early	obey their parents
do housework	live alone	~~wear pants~~

1. **A:** _Did women use to wear pants?_ _____

   B: No, they didn't. They used to wear dresses.

2. **A:** _____

   B: Yes, they did. There didn't use to be a lot of restaurants.

3. **A:** _____

   B: Yes, they did. They almost always listened to their parents.

4. **A:** _____

   B: No, they didn't. Housework was women's work.

5. **A:** _____

   B: No, they didn't. They lived with their families until they got married.

6. **A:** _____

   B: Yes, they did. They used to go to bed when the sun went down.

Grammar to Communicate 3:
Used to: Information Questions

A   Tina used to be a child tennis star. A reporter is asking her questions. Match the questions with the answers. Write the correct letters.

_f_ 1. Where did you use to train?   **a.** By plane.

____ 2. Who used to be your coach?   **b.** 5 or 6 hours a day.

____ 3. How did you use to travel to matches?   **c.** At night.

____ 4. How much did you use to practice?   **d.** I didn't have any!

____ 5. When did you use to study?   **e.** My dad.

____ 6. What did you use to do in your free time? **f.** ~~In Miami.~~

B   Ben is asking his grandmother questions about her life when she was young. Read her answers. Then write Ben's questions. Use *used to*.

1. **A:** _How much did movies use to cost?_
                    (cost)
   B: Movies? They only used to cost about 25 cents.

2. **A:** _____
                    (do)
   B: For fun? We used to listen to the radio or go to the movies.

3. **A:** _____
                    (get)
   B: To school? We used to walk.

4. **A:** _____
                    (work)
   B: I used to work at a department store.

5. **A:** _____
                    (make)
   B: I used to make $50 a week.

6. **A:** _____
                    (cost)
   B: An apartment downtown used to cost about $75 a month.

7. **A:** _____
                    (eat out)
   B: Are you kidding? We never ate out. I used to cook every day.

Review and Challenge

Find the mistake in each conversation. Circle the letter and correct the mistake.

1. **A:** I <u>used to</u> <u>made</u> my own clothes.   **Correct:** _____*make*_____
           A   (B)

    B: Really? Why <u>did</u> you <u>use to do</u> that?
                     C   D

2. **A:** We <u>didn't</u> <u>used to</u> have a car.   **Correct:** _____
             A   B

    B: Really? How <u>did you</u> <u>use to</u> get to work?
                       C   D

3. **A:** When <u>women used to</u> <u>get</u> married?   **Correct:** _____
                     A   B

    B: <u>They</u> <u>used to</u> get married at 16 or 17.
           C   D

4. **A:** <u>How</u> <u>people used to</u> heat their homes?   **Correct:** _____
           A   B

    B: They <u>used to</u> <u>make fires</u> in their fireplaces.
                C   D

5. **A:** <u>Who</u> <u>did use to</u> cook in your house?   **Correct:** _____
           A   B

    B: My father <u>did</u>. <u>He was</u> a very good cook.
                     C   D

6. **A:** My sister <u>used to be</u> a tennis player.   **Correct:** _____
                     A

    B: <u>Did you</u> <u>used to go</u> and <u>watch</u> her games?
           B   C   D

7. **A:** <u>Did she</u> <u>use to be</u> thin?   **Correct:** _____
           A   B

    B: No, she <u>wasn't</u>. She <u>was</u> heavy even when she was a child.
                   C   D

8. **A:** I <u>didn't use to</u> <u>like</u> my mother, but now <u>I am</u>.   **Correct:** _____
             A   B   C

    B: I still <u>don't get along with</u> mine!
                   D

9. **A:** We <u>didn't</u> <u>use argue</u> at all.   **Correct:** _____
             A   B

    B: My husband and I <u>didn't use</u> to <u>fight</u> either.
                            C   D

UNIT 6 VOCABULARY EXERCISES

A   Complete the conversations. Use the words in the box.

am free	answer the phone	get . . . to go
answer the door	~~drop . . . off~~	try out for

1. **Mary:**   Can you _____ *drop* _____ the children _____ *off* _____
   at school this morning?

   Jeff: No, I'm sorry—I can't. I have to go to work early.

2. **Timmy:**   Can you _____? I have to put the baby down.

   Jenny: I didn't hear the bell, but I'll check.

3. **Sandy:**   I'm going to _____ the basketball team at school.

   Jennifer: Good luck!

4. **Tim:**   What are we going to have for dinner?

   Karen: I'm going to _____ some fried chicken
   _____. I called the restaurant ten minutes ago, so it
   should be ready now.

5. **Rafael:**   I _____ tomorrow night. Will you go to the movies
   with me?

   Susan: Sure. I'd love to.

6. **Abdel:**   Can you _____, Lili? It's ringing.

   Lili: Sure. Where is it?

B   **Match the sentences. Write the correct letters.**

_d_   **1.** I rang the bell five times!

_____ **2.** Katya can't go to the movies.

_____ **3.** Jack's car is dirty.

_____ **4.** We don't have a car.

_____ **5.** Rafael has no food at home.

_____ **6.** I can't have lunch with you today.

_____ **7.** I need to take a shower, but Grandma is going to call us soon.

a. His father is going to help him wash it.

b. He's going to pick up some groceries at the supermarket.

c. Bill will give us a ride to the concert.

d. Why didn't you get the door?

e. Will you get the phone when it rings?

f. I'm going to attend a meeting from twelve to two o'clock.

g. She has to babysit her sister's children.

UNIT 6 GRAMMAR EXERCISES

Grammar to Communicate 1:
Future: *Will* for Decisions and Promises

A Read each conversation. Look at the underlined sentence. Write *D* for *decision* or *P* for *promise*.

_P_ 1. **Child:**   Waah!

   Dentist: Don't cry. <u>It won't hurt</u>.

____ 2. **Waitress:** We're out of the fish.

   Customer: OK. <u>I'll have the chicken</u>.

____ 3. **Client:**   I need to speak to Mr. Ho.

   Secretary: I'm sorry, but he isn't in today. <u>He'll call you tomorrow</u>.

____ 4. **Mother:**   Have fun, honey. <u>I'll pick you up later</u>.

   Son: OK, thanks. See you later!

____ 5. **Husband:**   Do you want me to get the phone?

   Wife: No, it's probably my sister. <u>I'll get it</u>.

____ 6. **Customer:** Is the problem serious?

   Mechanic: No. Come back in an hour. <u>Your car will be ready then</u>.

____ 7. **Waiter:**   What'll you have?

   Customer: <u>We'll both have the fish</u>.

B Complete the sentences. Use *'ll* or *won't* and the verbs in the box.

~~answer~~	be	get	give	help	hurt	tell

1. I _'ll answer_ the door. It's probably the babysitter.

2. He _____ you a ride. He has a car.

3. We don't have time to wait. We _____ somewhere to go.

4. I _____ anyone. It will be our secret.

5. Don't worry. I _____ you finish.

6. He's sorry. He _____ you again. He promised.

7. We _____ late. We promise.

Grammar to Communicate 2:
Future: *Be going to* and *Will*

A   **Complete each conversation. Circle the correct answer. Write it on the line.**

1. **A:** So, what are your son's plans for next year?

    B: _____He is going to_____ take two courses at the community college.
           (He is going to / He'll)

2. **A:** I need help. These boxes are so heavy!

    B: I have a truck. _____ help you move.
            (I'm going to / I'll)

3. **A:** Sheila and I _____ meet at the library later. Would
            (are going to / will)
            you like to come?

    B: No, thank you. I'm busy.

4. **A:** Tom _____ try out for the play this year.
            (isn't going to / won't)

    B: Really? Why not?

5. **A:** The party is a surprise, so please don't tell anyone.

    B: Don't worry. _____ say a word.
            (We're not going to / We won't)

6. **A:** I'm free on Saturday night. Do you want to do something?

    B: Sure. _____ give you a call.
            (I'm going to / I'll)

B   **Complete Lynn's note to her roommate Julie. Use *will* or *be going to*.**

Hi Julie,

    I _'m going to be_____ away all next week on a business trip. My
         1. (be)

mother _____ the cats for me. I hope that's OK with you. I
        2. (feed)

talked to her and she _____ during the day when you're at
        3. (come)

work. I promise that she _____ you like she did last time!
        4. (not bother)

Oh, and the landlord _____ the apartment on Tuesday, so
        5. (show)

please make sure everything is neat. I _____ you next week!
        6. (see)

Lynn

Grammar to Communicate 3:
Future: Present Progressive for Future Arrangements

A Look at Bert and Melissa's calendar for next week. Complete the sentences. (Be careful! Some are affirmative, and some are negative.)

MONDAY	TUESDAY	WEDNESDAY	THURSDAY	FRIDAY	SATURDAY	SUNDAY
Holiday!!	M: doctor - 2:00	B: softball 7-9? P.M. M: dinner w/ Holly	B: breakfast meeting	M: 4:00 haircut with Jacques	B's parents!!	

1. They ____*aren't working*____ on Monday. It's a holiday.
   (work)
2. Melissa ____*is leaving*____ work early on Tuesday for a doctor's appointment.
   (leave)
3. Bert _____ softball on Wednesday evening.
   (play)
4. Melissa _____ him up after the game because she
   (pick)
   _____ dinner with Holly.
   (have)
5. Bert _____ a breakfast meeting on Thursday morning.
   (attend)
6. Melissa _____ her hair cut on Friday afternoon.
   (get)
7. Bert's parents _____ over on Saturday.
   (come)

B Complete the conversations about Bert and Melissa's schedule. Read the answers. Then complete the questions.

1. **A:** How many days ____*are they working*____ next week?
   B: They're working four days next week.

2. **A:** What time _____ the doctor on Tuesday?
   B: She's seeing the doctor at 2:00.

3. **A:** _____ softball on Wednesday morning?
   B: No, he isn't. He's playing on Wednesday evening.

4. **A:** What _____ on Thursday morning?
   B: He's attending a meeting.

5. **A:** Who _____ Melissa's hair on Friday?
   B: Jacques is.

6. **A:** _____ on Sunday?
   B: No, they aren't. They're visiting on Saturday.

Review and Challenge

Complete each sentence. Circle the letter of the correct answer.

1. I'd like to go to Marta's party on Sunday, but _____.

    a. I'm working.   **b.** I'll work

2. Our flight _____ after midnight. You don't need to pick us up.

    a. is arriving   **b.** will arrive

3. We _____ be late again. We promise.

    a. aren't going to   **b.** won't

4. It's a beautiful day. I think _____ a walk.

    a. I'm taking   **b.** I'll take

5. Don't worry about it. Your parents _____ you pay for it. They promised.

    a. are helping   **b.** will help

6. _____ answer the phone, please? I'm in the shower.

    a. Are you going to   **b.** Will you

7. So, have you registered yet? How many courses _____ next semester?

    a. are you going to take   **b.** will you take

8. _____ anything on Saturday night?

    a. Are you doing   **b.** Will you do

9. _____ a cup of coffee, please.

    a. I'm going to have   **b.** I'll have

10. Stephanie _____ for us on Friday. She has a game.

    a. isn't babysitting   **b.** won't babysit

UNIT 7 VOCABULARY EXERCISES

A Complete the sentences about Alex. Use the words in the box.

apply for	gets good grades	take an exam
gets a scholarship	major in	~~transfer~~

1. Alex is going to _____transfer_____ to Wellington University after two years at his community college.

2. If Alex _____ this semester, he will have an excellent transcript.

3. If Alex _____, he won't have to pay for the university.

4. If Alex doesn't win the award, he's going to _____ a job.

5. He is going to _____ English. It's his favorite subject.

6. Alex will _____ on Monday for Wellington University.

B Complete the sentences about Steve. Use the words in the box.

cheat	improve	~~take three courses~~
failed the class	pass the class	takes the finals

1. Steve is going to ___take three courses___ this term: Spanish, algebra, and English.

2. Steve took Spanish last year too, but he _____. He was very disappointed.

3. Steve has to _____ this time if he wants to graduate.

4. If Steve's grades _____ before the end of the term, he will have a good transcript for college.

5. If he _____ and fails, he won't get into a good college.

6. Even if he doesn't study for his exams, he won't _____ on them because he might get kicked out of school.

UNIT 7 GRAMMAR EXERCISES

Grammar to Communicate 1:
Future: *If* Clauses for Possibility

A   **Complete each sentence. Circle the correct answer.**

1. If I don't pass the course, I _____ it again next semester.

    a. take   **(b.)** will take   **c.** going to take

2. If you _____ late again, I'm going to tell the principal.

    a. are   **b.** will be   **c.** are going to be

3. He won't transfer to that school if they _____ him a scholarship.

    a. don't give   **b.** doesn't give   **c.** gives

4. If she gets a scholarship, her parents _____ very happy.

    a. are   **b.** will be   **c.** is going to be

5. You _____ if you don't study.

    a. don't pass   **b.** will pass   **c.** aren't going to pass

6. If we _____ for a scholarship, we will never get one.

    a. don't apply   **b.** not apply   **c.** won't apply

7. They _____ five courses next semester if they do well this semester.

    a. take   **b.** are taking   **c.** are going to take

B   **Write ✓ if the sentence is correct. Write ✗ if it is incorrect. Then correct the
incorrect sentences.**

___✓___ **1.** I'm going to go to Birch College if they give me a scholarship.

                                                going to graduate
___✗___ **2.** If he fails the final exam, he's not ~~graduate~~.

___·___ **3.** You won't learn anything if you will cheat.

_____ **4.** If they get good grades this semester, they are going to transfer to a

              better university.

_____ **5.** If I won't do well in my math classes, I am not going to major in math.

_____ **6.** If you are absent on the day of the make-up test, I give you an F.

_____ **7.** We'll help you pay for university if you aren't get a scholarship.

Grammar to Communicate 2:
Future: Time Clauses

A Read each sentence. Then write *1* next to the event that will happen first. Write *2* next to the event that will happen second.

1. Collette will look for a job after she graduates.

   _2_ She'll look for a job.
   _1_ She'll graduate.

2. She won't look for a job until she graduates.

   ____ She'll look for a job.
   ____ She'll graduate.

3. She isn't going to apply to college until she saves enough money.

   ____ She's going to apply to college.
   ____ She's going to save enough money.

4. Before she applies to college, she's going to work for a year.

   ____ She's going to apply to college.
   ____ She's going to work for a year.

5. When the colleges see her excellent grades, they will accept her.

   ____ The colleges will see her excellent grades.
   ____ They will accept her.

6. As soon as she gets accepted to college, she's going to quit her job.

   ____ She is going to get accepted to college.
   ____ She is going to quit her job.

7. She won't quit her job until she gets an acceptance letter.

   ____ She will quit her job.
   ____ She will get an acceptance letter.

B Complete the paragraph. Some sentences have more than one correct answer.

I'm 40 years old. I got married and had children when I was very young. I never had the chance to go to college. But now my kids are teenagers, so it's my turn. As soon as my youngest son ____starts____ high
    1. (start)
school, I _____ for classes at the community college. I
          2. (register)
_____ classes there until my son _____ high
        3. (take)   4. (finish)
school. After he _____, I _____ to the state
                   5. (graduate)   6. (apply)
university. I'm not sure what I will major in. I _____ for at least
                                                      7. (study)
a year before I _____ a major. I've waited more than 20 years for
                   8. (choose)
this moment, so I want to make the right decision.

NAME: _____   DATE: _____

Grammar to Communicate 3:
Future: *May* and *Might* for Possibility

A Complete the sentences. Circle the correct answer. Write it on the line.

1. It looks cloudy. Where's my umbrella? It _____*might*_____ rain later.
    (will / ⓜ️might)

2. I _____ get in, but I'm going to apply anyway. You never know!
    (might not /won't)

3. You failed all of your courses. You _____ graduate. I'm sorry.
    (are not going to / may not)

4. He's the best student in the school. I'm sure that he _____
    (will / might)
    get a scholarship.

5. Maybe I _____ take some classes at night.
    (will / might)

6. They _____ move. They don't know yet.
    (will / may)

7. Perhaps we _____ get an apartment together.
    (will / may)

B Complete the conversation. Use *may, might, be going to* or *will*. Some sentences have more than one correct answer.

Bob: I _*'m going to get*_ a job this summer. I need money for college.
          1 (get)

Al: Well, I applied to the state college, but my grades aren't very good, so I

          _____ in.
          2. (not get)

Bob: So what are you going to do if they don't accept you?

Al: I don't know. I _____ at my father's construction
          3. (work)
          company.

Bob: Oh, really? Maybe your father _____ me a job, too!
          4. (give)

Al: He _____ that. I _____ him for
          5. (do)   6. (ask)
          you.

Bob: Really? Thanks a lot! Hey, Jim and I _____ a movie
          7. (see)
          tonight. Do you want to come?

Al: Sure.

Bob: OK. We _____ you up at 8:00.
          8. (pick)

Review and Challenge

Find the mistake in each conversation. Circle the letter and correct the mistake.

1. **A:** I <u>might</u> <u>to be</u> late tomorrow.
         A   (B)

   Correct: _____*be*_____

   B: But <u>we're</u> <u>having</u> a test!
         C   D

2. **A:** I don't feel well. <u>Maybe</u> <u>I'll</u> <u>stay home</u>.
                  A   B   C

   Correct: _____

   B: Your teacher <u>might don't</u> like that.
                    D

3. **A:** I'm not <u>going leave</u> until he <u>calls</u>.
              A   B

   Correct: _____

   B: But if we <u>don't leave</u> right now, <u>we're</u> going to miss our plane!
               C   D

4. **A:** It <u>might rain</u> tomorrow.
          A

   Correct: _____

   B: Really? Well, <u>perhaps</u> <u>we'll be</u> lucky and it <u>doesn't rain</u>.
              B   C   D

5. **A:** He <u>might</u> <u>not be</u> the right person for the job.
         A   B

   Correct: _____

   B: But if we <u>don't give</u> him a chance, we <u>never know</u>.
              C   D

6. **A:** He <u>maybe transfer</u> next year.
           A

   Correct: _____

   B: Really? I <u>might transfer</u> too. <u>I'll decide</u> when <u>I get</u> my grades.
             B   C   D

7. **A:** If your work <u>not improve</u>, <u>you're going</u> <u>to fail</u>.
              A   B   C

   Correct: _____

   B: Don't worry. <u>I'll pass</u>. I'm sure.
             D

8. **A:** You <u>might</u> <u>don't get</u> the scholarship.
         A   B

   Correct: _____

   B: That's OK. If I <u>don't get</u> it, <u>I'll apply</u> for another one.
               C   D

9. **A:** <u>Until</u> we <u>finish</u> our exams, we're going to take a vacation.
      A   B

   Correct: _____

   B: Where <u>are you</u> <u>going to go</u>?
            C   D

10. **A:** When <u>are you</u> <u>going to make</u> your decision?
            A   B

   Correct: _____

   B: <u>We'll decide</u> <u>soon as we look</u> at all of the applications.
        C   D

UNIT 8 VOCABULARY EXERCISES

A Complete the job advertisements. Use the words in the box.

~~cash register~~	the day shift	overtime	train
contact	the night shift	search	

WANTED: CASHIER

We are looking for a good worker for our convenience store. We prefer someone who has experience with a _____cash register_____, but if you

1.

don't know how it works, we will _____ you. This

2.

position is for _____, from 7 A.M. to 4 P.M. If you are

3.

interested, please _____ Mrs. Sanchez at 555-1234.

4.

WANTED: BAKER

Do you like to bake? Do you like to have your days free? If your answer is "yes," don't _____ any more! This is the job for you.

5.

Please come in person to Bellini's Restaurant on Monday afternoon to apply. You will work from 6 P.M. to 2 A.M. This is _____.

6.

You will work forty hours a week. However, we may ask you to work

_____ on Saturdays or Sundays for extra pay.

7.

B   **Complete the sentences. Use the words in the box.**

fired	heard from	~~owned~~
handled	hired	quit

1. Rema worked for herself. She _____*owned*_____ a bookstore.

2. Marcel didn't like his job as assistant manager at the car wash, so he
   _____.

3. Dennis had a job at a bank. He _____ money all day.

4. After Jack took money from the cash register, he was _____.

5. Lotte had a great interview, so she was _____ to work at the hair
   salon.

6. Ann went to the employment agency to look for a job last week, but she hasn't
   _____ them yet.

UNIT 8 GRAMMAR EXERCISES

Grammar to Communicate 1:
Present Perfect: Regular Verbs

A **Complete the sentences. Use *has*, *hasn't*, *have*, or *haven't*.**

1. I ____have____ never attended a job fair.

2. Lucille _____ ever contacted an employment agency.

3. Bertha and Ruth _____ never talked to a job counselor.

4. Andrea _____ never worked with children.

5. My parents _____ ever helped me find a job.

6. We _____ never asked our parents for help.

7. That company _____ ever hired a female manager.

B **Amy has graduated from college and is starting a job search. Read her list. Then write sentences about what she *has* and *hasn't* done.**

finish my résumé
post my résumé online
✓ look in the Sunday newspaper
contact an employment agency
✓ talk to the job counselor at school
✓ register for a computer course

1. _She hasn't finished her résumé._____

2. _____

3. _____

4. _____

5. _____

6. _____

Grammar to Communicate 2:
Present Perfect: Irregular Verbs

A **Read each comment. Check the correct box.**

	Searching for a worker	Searching for a job
1. We've hired an employment agency, but they haven't found us anyone yet.	✓	☐
2. He's spoken to an employment agency, but he hasn't gone on any interviews yet.	☐	☐
3. The employment agency has already sent us several résumés.	☐	☐
4. He hasn't left yet, but he will soon. We need to hire someone before he leaves.	☐	☐
5. I haven't quit yet. I want to find another job first.	☐	☐
6. She's sent them her résumé, but she hasn't heard from them yet.	☐	☐
7. They've decided to post the job online. They want a lot of people to apply.	☐	☐

B **Complete the sentences. Use the present perfect. (Be careful! Some are affirmative, and some are negative.)**

1. I _____*haven't heard*_____ from the manager yet. If I don't hear from her this
   (hear)
   week, I'll call her again.

2. Mr. Hook _____ your résumé yet. He won't contact you until
   (get)
   he gets it.

3. I think that someone _____ the job already. I'll call you if it's
   (take)
   still available.

4. I _____ your résumé to my boss. He'll call you if he is
   (give)
   interested.

5. We _____ your résumé yet. We can't schedule an interview
   (see)
   until we see it.

6. He _____ a job already. But we'll help you find someone else.
   (find)

Grammar to Communicate 3:
Present Perfect: *Yes / No* Questions

A   Match the questions with the answers. Write the correct letters.

_b_ **1.** Have you ever worked the night shift?

2. Have you had any experience as a manager?

3. Have you told your boss that you're leaving?

4. Has your boss ever given you a bad review?

5. Have you ever had a problem with the police?

6. Has your boss ever asked you to work overtime?

7. Has another company offered you a job?

a. No, I haven't. I haven't told him yet.

b. ~~Yes, I have, but I prefer to work days.~~

c. No, but I've taken management classes.

d. No, but I'm happy to work extra hours.

e. No, he hasn't. He's happy with my work.

f. Not yet, but I've had several interviews.

g. No, of course not! I've always obeyed the law.

B   Write questions. Put the words into the correct order.

1. Has he had a lot of interviews?
_____
      (he / had / a lot of / has / interviews)

2. _____
      (a job/ you / applied for / have / here / ever)

3. _____
      (they / ever / fired / have / an employee)

4. _____
      (she / finished / has / the training program)

5. _____
      (ever / owned / your / you / have / own business)

6. _____
      (you / handled / have / large amounts of / money / ever)

7. _____
      (used / a cash register / has / ever / he)

Review and Challenge

Complete the letter. Use the words in the box. (Be careful! There are extra words.)

~~already~~	ever	hasn't	have	yet
be	had	he	haven't	you
been	has	he's	never	you've

Dear Mom and Dad,

Well, I've ___*already*___ gone on several interviews, but I _____
                    1.   2.

found a job yet. Dad, your friend from the employment agency _____
                                                                    3.

contacted me. Maybe _____ been busy. When you have time, will you
                         4.

call him? Thanks.

Mom, Aunt Mary has left me three messages, but I haven't _____
                                                              5.

time to call her _____. Have you talked to her? If she calls, please
                     6.

tell her that I'll call as soon as I get a chance. You know how she is. She's

_____ been very patient!
    7.

The weather here _____ been perfect. I haven't seen much of the
                     8.

city, but it really is very nice. I know _____ been here in the summer,
                                              9.

but have you _____ been here in the spring? You have to come for a
                  10.

visit. I know you'll love it, and of course I would love to see you. Think about

it, OK?

I miss you! Write soon!

Love,

Lisa

UNIT 9 VOCABULARY EXERCISES

A   Complete the story. Use the words in the box.

argued	fights	honeymoon	~~remarried~~	widow

Maria is so happy these days. She is getting _____remarried_____ soon to Rodrigo. She has been a _____ since her last husband, Gordon, died.

1.

2.

She is going to San Juan for the _____. She

3.

never _____ with Rodrigo. Actually, they

4.

haven't _____ once since they've been

5.

together.

B   Complete the conversation. Use the words in the box.

birth	~~broke up~~	marriage	newlyweds	widower

Setting: Raisa's wedding. Two guests, Sandy and Caroline, are talking during a wedding ceremony.

Sandy: Look at Nancy over there with her new boyfriend! She
_____broke up_____ with her last boyfriend two days ago!

1.

Caroline: That's terrible! By the way, did you hear about Raisa's parents?

Sandy: Yes. They don't have a good _____. They aren't even

2.

sitting together.

Caroline: There's Carl. His wife died last year, and now he's a _____.

3.

Sandy: He's handsome. I saw him at the party to celebrate the

_____ of Bob and Susan's baby daughter.

4.

Caroline: Look at Trey and Rosie. They are _____. They were

5.

married last week.

Sandy: Wow! They're a cute couple!

UNIT 9 GRAMMAR EXERCISES

Grammar to Communicate 1:
Present Perfect: *For* and *Since*

A **Read each situation. Then complete each sentence. Write *for* or *since*.**

1. Paul got divorced a year ago. He has been divorced ____*for*____ a year.

2. Jen gave birth two months ago. She has been a mother _____ May.

3. Deb and Sue are getting along. They haven't had a fight _____ a while.

4. Ron moved to a new city a month ago. He hasn't made any friends _____ his move.

5. Andy's wife died last year. He has been a widower _____ a year.

B **Read the situations. Write one sentence with *since* and one with *for*.**

1. Mia and Dan are on their honeymoon. They arrived at the hotel on Sunday. It is Wednesday.
   a. Mia and Dan have been on their honeymoon ____*since Sunday*____.
   b. They've been on their honeymoon ____*for four days*____.

2. Rafael and Diana got married ten years ago. After nine years of marriage, they separated and Rafael got his own apartment.
   a. Rafael and Diana haven't lived together _____.
   b. They haven't lived together _____.

3. Justin got divorced in February. It's November, and he's not dating anyone.
   a. Justin has been single _____.
   b. He's been single _____.

4. Gerry and Alice are best friends. They met in kindergarten. They are middle-aged.
   a. Gerry and Alice have known each other _____.
   b. They've known each other _____.

5. Ann had a baby three months ago, in September. She quit her job in July.
   a. Ann hasn't worked _____.
   b. She hasn't worked _____.

Grammar to Communicate 2:
Present Perfect Progressive: *For* and *Since*

A   Complete the affirmative and negative sentences. Use the present perfect progressive of the verbs in the box and *for* or *since*.

date	get along	live alone	spend	stay	wait

1. We started going out two months ago. We <u>'ve been dating for</u> two months.

2. I moved into my own apartment a year ago. I really like having my own place. I _____ a year.

3. My sister and her husband started arguing every day last year. My sister _____ with her husband _____ last year.

4. Mr. Johnson started a new job in May. He used to do a lot of things with his family, but now he works 80 hours a week. Mr. Johnson _____ any time with his family _____ May.

5. Belle's boyfriend said that he would pick her up at 8:00. It's 9:30, and he hasn't arrived. Belle _____ an hour and a half.

6. Mr. and Mrs. Matthews separated in February, and Mr. Matthews moved in with his mother. It's August, and he's still living with his mother. He _____ with his mother _____ February.

B   Write ✓ if the sentence is correct. Write ✗ if it is incorrect. Then correct the incorrect sentences.

__✓__ 1. I've been talking for 10 minutes, but you haven't been listening.

'*ve been waiting*
__✗__ 2. Where have you been? I'm waiting for an hour!

_____ 3. My roommate and I have been living together since a month.

_____ 4. They have been knowing each other since high school.

_____ 5. I haven't heard from Pat for several months. I've been dating someone else.

_____ 6. They've been spending a lot of time together since his divorce.

_____ 7. She is not been sleeping very well since her son's birth.

Grammar to Communicate 3:
Present Perfect Progressive: Questions

A Dan is asking Ruth about her boyfriend, Bill. Match the questions with the answers. Write the correct letters.

_d_ **1.** Why have you been thinking about it?

2. Has he been going out with other girls?

3. What have you been arguing about?

4. How long have you known each other?

5. Have you been dating other guys?

a. We've been friends since childhood.

b. Everything! Maybe we've been together for too long.

c. No, but I've been thinking about it!

d. Because Bill and I haven't been getting along.

e. Maybe. He hasn't been spending much time with me lately.

B Complete the conversations. Write questions. Use the present perfect progressive.

1. A: How long have you been living here?
   _____
   (how long /you / live here)

  B: For about two years.

2. A: _____
   (how long / you / look for / a roommate)

  B: Just a couple of days. I put the ad in the paper on Sunday.

3. A: _____
   (you / get / a lot of calls)

  B: Yes, we have. The phone's been ringing all day!

4. A: _____
   (your other roommates / help / you)

  B: Yes, of course. We've all been answering the phone.

5. A: _____
   (how long / the landlord / rent / this apartment)

  B: For a long time. The tenants before us were here for 15 years.

6. A: _____ It looks great.
   (the landlord / work / on the place / recently)

  B: Yes, he has. I think that he's been getting ready to increase the rent!

Review and Challenge

Correct the conversation. There are ten mistakes. The first mistake is corrected for you.

Rachel: Betsy, what's wrong? You look terrible.

Betsy: Lately Danny and I haven't been getting along.

Rachel: I'm sorry to hear that. How long have you ∧*been* having problems?

Betsy: Since a few months. But it is been getting a lot worse recently.

Rachel: What do you mean?

Betsy: Well, Danny's been stayed out late almost every night. He no been spending any time with me or the kids lately.

Rachel: What do you mean? He has been working late?

Betsy: He says that he has, but I don't believe him.

Rachel: Why not?

Betsy: I don't know. It's just a feeling.

Rachel: How long you and Danny are married?

Betsy: For 15 years. We're together since high school.

Rachel: And has he ever lying to you?

Betsy: No, he hasn't never lied to me.

Rachel: Then why don't you believe him now?

Betsy: Hmm . . . Maybe you have a point.

UNIT 10 VOCABULARY EXERCISES

A Complete the conversation. Use the words in the box.

attractive	calm	clear	fashionable	successful	~~terrific~~

Margo: Have you noticed how different Greta and Janet are on the TV show, *Office Life*?

Lena: Yes. Greta is a terrible employee, but Janet is a _____terrific_____ employee!
                                                                    1.

Margo: And Janet is a very _____ salesperson. She sells a lot of
                                        2.
products.

Lena: Greta doesn't sell anything! Maybe it's because she's very difficult to

understand on the phone. Her voice isn't _____, like
                                                          3.
Janet's.

Margo: Greta gets excited and talks too fast. She should try to be

_____ and relaxed.
              4.

Lena: You know, I feel a little sorry for Greta. She's ugly and her clothes are twenty

years old.

Margo: I know! Janet is the opposite. She has a very _____ face.
                                                                    5.

Lena: And Janet's clothes are _____ , too. She looks like a model
                                              6.
from a magazine.

B   **Complete the sentences. Use the words in the box.**

awful	~~nervous~~	romantic	secret	star	strange

1. Jack was not prepared for his presentation. He felt very _____*nervous*_____.

2. When he was at work, Elise left a _____ gift on the table for her husband.

3. It was a _____ movie. Elephants danced and fought aliens with cookies.

4. On Valentines' Day, Jerry was going to give his girlfriend flowers, but he decided a necklace was more _____.

5. The job interview was _____. I couldn't remember the manager's name and forgot to bring my résumé.

6. My favorite movie _____ is Cate Blanchett. She is very graceful.

UNIT 10 GRAMMAR EXERCISES

Grammar to Communicate 1:
Adverbs and Adjectives

A Underline the adjective in each sentence. Then write its adverb form.

1. The star of the show is a <u>good</u> dancer.   _____well_____

2. She is a bad actress.   _____

3. Movie stars are attractive dressers.   _____

4. Television chefs are usually neat.   _____

5. On police shows, the officers are fast drivers.   _____

6. The director is a hard worker.   _____

7. That actor is a slow learner.   _____

B Rewrite the sentences in Exercise A. Use the adverb. Keep the same meaning.

1. <u>The star of the show dances well.</u>
                         (dance)

2. _____
                         (act)

3. _____
                         (dress)

4. _____
                         (cook)

5. _____
                         (drive)

6. _____
                         (work)

7. _____
                         (learn)

NAME: _____ DATE: _____

Grammar to Communicate 2:
Adverbs of Manner

 A **Read the sentences. Answer the questions. Use an adverb.**

1. That actor has a strange voice. How does he speak?
   <u>He speaks strangely.</u>

2. Police officers have dangerous lives. How do they live?

3. That child is polite. How is he behaving?

4. The newlyweds are having a romantic conversation. How are they talking?

5. That actress has a very soft voice. How does she speak?

6. I am a nervous driver. How do I drive?

7. Her clothes are fashionable. How does she dress?

B **Complete the sentences. Use an adjective or adverb in the box. (Be careful! There are extra words.)**

angry / angrily	clear / clearly	noisy / noisily	successful / successfully
awful / awfully	easy / ~~easily~~	soft / softly	terrific / terrifically

1. It is hard for him to learn. He doesn't learn ___easily___.
2. He is an _____ cook. His food doesn't taste good.
3. They are making a lot of noise. They aren't talking _____.
4. He doesn't speak _____. I can't understand him easily.
5. You're wrong! She doesn't sound _____! She is a terrible singer.
6. They are famous actors. They have acted in several _____ movies.
7. The director is very calm. He doesn't look _____.

Grammar to Communicate 3:
Adverbs of Degree

A Complete each sentence. Circle the correct answer. Write it on the line.

1. That movie was five hours long. It was ___extremely___ long.
   (pretty / (extremely))

2. That movie was 90 minutes long. It was _____ short.
   (pretty / extremely)

3. He is the best-looking actor I've ever seen. He is _____ attractive.
   (pretty / really)

4. That director has directed one successful movie. He is _____
   (pretty / very)
   successful.

5. The woman is trying out for a part in a television show. She's never tried
   out for anything before. She's _____ nervous.
   (pretty / very)

6. You watched a sitcom on TV. You laughed a few times. It was
   _____ funny.
   (pretty / really)

7. You watched the news in English. You understood everything. They were
   speaking _____ clearly.
   (pretty / very)

B Write ✓ if the underlined part of the sentence is correct. Write X if it is
incorrect. Then correct the incorrect sentences.

really or extremely
___X___ 1. He's a terrific cook. He cooks <u>pretty well</u>.

___✓___ 2. It's not the best show on television, but it's <u>pretty good</u>.

_____ 3. Has she been sick? She looks <u>very terrible</u>.

_____ 4. He never makes a mistake. He does everything <u>very perfectly</u>.

_____ 5. The acting on that show is <u>extremely awful</u>.

_____ 6. She sings <u>extremely well</u>.

_____ 7. That reporter speaks <u>pretty quickly</u>. I can't understand anything that
   he says!

Review and Challenge

Find the mistake in each item. Circle the letter and correct the mistake.

1. Movie actors usually act <u>real</u> <u>well</u>, but many
                     (A) B

   soap opera stars are <u>pretty</u> <u>bad</u> actors.
                  C   D

   Correct: _____really_____

2. <u>Good</u> talk show hosts interview <u>people interesting</u>
     A   B

   and ask <u>really</u> <u>excellent</u> questions.
            C   D

   Correct: _____

3. <u>Really</u> <u>popularly</u> television shows sometimes
     A   B

   continue for <u>a very</u> <u>long</u> time.
            C   D

   Correct: _____

4. That show was <u>very</u> <u>awful</u>, and the tickets were
              A   B

   <u>extremely</u> <u>expensive</u>!
     C   D

   Correct: _____

5. Chef Rick's cakes always <u>look</u> <u>beautiful</u>, but they
                     A   B

   taste <u>pretty</u> <u>terribly</u>.
       C   D

   Correct: _____

6. What are they saying? I can't <u>well hear</u> because
                        A

   they <u>are speaking</u> <u>very</u> <u>softly</u>.
        B   C   D

   Correct: _____

7. That police show is always <u>extremely</u> <u>exciting</u>.
                  A   B

   It's never <u>slowly</u> or <u>boring</u>.
          C   D

   Correct: _____

8. Everyone was laughing <u>really</u> <u>hardly</u>. The show
                  A   B

   was <u>extremely</u> <u>funny</u>.
       C   D

   Correct: _____

9. Please be <u>quietly</u>. You're <u>very</u> <u>noisy</u>, and I can't
         A   B   C

   hear the television <u>very well</u>.
                 D

   Correct: _____

UNIT 11 VOCABULARY EXERCISES

 A   **Read about a zoo tour. Complete the paragraphs. Use the words in the box.**

chimpanzees	dolphins	elephant	~~lions~~	rabbits

Jackson Zoo

Welcome to the Jackson Zoo. We have many animals here. Do you see the

_____lions_____ under the tree? These big cats come from Africa. On
1.

the right is an _____, one of the biggest animals on the planet.
2.

And look in the trees! Do you see the _____? They are playful
3.

and move very quickly.

The sea animal show begins at 11:00. This show includes

_____—some of the most beautiful animals. They are very
4.

intelligent, too.

The small animals get the fewest visitors, but they are interesting. I like the

_____ the best. They are very cute.
5.

B   **Match the definitions with the animals. Write the correct letters.**

_g_ 1. These are some of the largest animals. They live in the ocean.

____ 2. These birds live in cold places. They don't fly—they swim!

____ 3. These animals fly, but they aren't birds. They are awake at night.

____ 4. These animals live in the desert. They may live for six months without water.

____ 5. These stubborn animals are like horses, but they are smaller.

____ 6. These large animals are dangerous when they are angry. They sleep in the winter.

____ 7. These small animals live in cities. They frighten a lot of people.

a. camels

b. bears

c. donkeys

d. rats

e. bats

f. penguins

~~**g.**~~ whales

UNIT 11 GRAMMAR EXERCISES

Grammar to Communicate 1:
Comparative and Superlative of Adjectives and Adverbs

A Complete the sentences. Use the comparative of the words in the box. Use each word only once.

~~dangerous~~ far good heavy quietly small

1. Bears are _more dangerous than_ donkeys.

2. Chimps climb trees _____ bears.

3. A whale is _____ a lion.

4. A snake can move _____ a pig.

5. A falcon can see _____ a bat.

6. Rabbits are _____ chimps.

B Compare the animals. Use the superlative.

1. _____Whales live the longest._____
   (live / long)

2. _____
   (have / short lives)

3. _____
   (be / stubborn)

4. _____
   (swim / quickly)

5. _____
   (can be trained / easy)

6. _____
   (be / heavy)

Grammar to Communicate 2:
Comparative and Superlative of Nouns

A **Complete the sentences about the zoo. Use the comparative or superlative.**

1. The lions are the biggest meat eaters. The lions eat ____the most meat____ .
    (meat)

2. The elephants need a lot of space. They need ____more space than____ the lions.
    (space)

3. The chimps are the most playful animals of all. The chimps spend

    _____ playing.
    (time)

4. All of the animals play except for the snakes. The snakes spend

    _____ playing.
    (time)

5. The parrots are noisier than the penguins. The penguins make

    _____ the parrots.
    (noise)

6. More people visit the gorillas than the bears. The bears have

    _____ the gorillas.
    (visitors)

7. The bats sleep almost all day, but they don't sleep much at night. Of all the

    animals in the zoo, the bats sleep _____ a night.
    (hours)

B **Look at the information about three national parks in Africa. Write comparative or superlative sentences.**

	ADDO ELEPHANT PARK, SOUTH AFRICA	KRUGER NATIONAL PARK, SOUTH AFRICA	CHOBE NATIONAL PARK, BOTSWANA
NUMBER OF ELEPHANTS	400	11,000	120,000
SPACE	1,600 square kilometers	20,000 square kilometers	11,000 square kilometers
VISITORS/YEAR	140,000	over 1 million	56,000

1. (Addo / has / elephants / of the three) _Addo has the fewest elephants of the three._

2. (Chobe / elephants/ Kruger) _____

3. (Chobe / has / space/ Kruger) _____

4. (Addo / has / space / of the three) _____

5. (Chobe / has / visitors/ Addo) _____

6. (Kruger / has / visitors / of the three) _____

7. (Kruger / has / elephants / Chobe) _____

Grammar to Communicate 3: Equatives

A **Read each sentence. Circle the letter of the sentence with the same meaning.**

1. Cats don't need as much attention as dogs do.
    a. Cats and dogs need the same amount of attention.
    b. Cats need less attention than dogs do. *(circled)*

2. Fish aren't as noisy as birds.
    a. Fish don't make as much noise as birds.
    b. Birds are the noisiest of all pets.

3. Rabbits need as much space as cats.
    a. Rabbits and cats need the same amount of space.
    b. Rabbits need more space than cats.

4. Parrots are as intelligent as dogs.
    a. Dogs are as intelligent as parrots.
    b. Parrots are more intelligent than dogs.

5. Cats do not obey their owners as well as dogs do.
    a. Cats are more obedient than dogs are.
    b. Dogs obey their owners better than cats do.

6. Cats aren't as messy as birds.
    a. Cats are neater than birds.
    b. Cats aren't as neat as birds.

B **Rewrite the sentences. Use *not as . . . as*. Keep the same meaning.**

1. My cat is cleaner than my parrot.   My parrot isn't as clean as my cat.

2. My dog can walk farther than my cat. _____

3. My parrot cost more than my cat did. _____

4. My parrot sings better than I do.   _____

5. I need less sleep than my cat does.   _____

6. My cat is cuter than my dogs are.   _____

NAME: _____ DATE: _____

Review and Challenge

Find the mistake in each sentence. Circle the letter and correct the mistake.

1. Cats <u>are</u> <u>good</u> pets <u>than</u> birds <u>are</u>.
       A   (B)   C   D

   Correct: ___*better*___

2. Dogs need <u>as</u> <u>many</u> <u>love</u> <u>as</u> children.
              A   B   C D

   Correct: _____

3. Gorillas are <u>more</u> <u>heavier</u> and <u>taller</u> <u>than</u> chimps.
                 A   B   C   D

   Correct: _____

4. A dog <u>isn't</u> <u>as</u> <u>intelligent</u> <u>than</u> a gorilla is.
           A B   C   D

   Correct: _____

5. Elephants <u>are</u> <u>the</u> <u>bigger</u> land <u>animals</u>.
             A   B   C   D

   Correct: _____

6. Cats <u>don't</u> learn <u>as</u> <u>easier</u> <u>as</u> dogs.
          A   B   C D

   Correct: _____

7. There <u>are</u> <u>less</u> <u>dogs</u> in my country <u>than</u> in the United States.
          A B   C   D

   Correct: _____

8. Dolphins can swim <u>more</u> <u>quick</u> <u>than</u> people <u>can</u>.
                  A   B   C   D

   Correct: _____

9. The zoo had <u>fewest</u> <u>visitors</u> <u>last year</u> <u>than the year</u> before.
              A   B   C   D

   Correct: _____

10. Snails <u>move</u> <u>the</u> <u>slower</u> <u>of</u> all animals.
           A   B   C   D

    Correct: _____

UNIT 12 VOCABULARY EXERCISES

 A   Look at the picture. Complete the sentences. Use the words in the box.

enjoying

herself

~~ordering~~

salad bar

seating

serving

specials

treating

1. Jeff is _____ordering_____ food from a waitress.

2. Susan is _____ Deb and Ken.

3. The _____ for today are on a sign behind Susan.

4. Maggie is _____.

5. Jenny is helping herself at the _____.

6. Sara is _____ food to customers.

7. Kako is _____ her friend to lunch.

B Complete the conversation. Use the words in the box.

appetizers	help themselves	napkins
dessert	~~main dish~~	stuff themselves

Hiroko: I'm making an American Thanksgiving dinner this week. I'm making turkey

for the _____main dish_____.
1.

Martha: Are you making pie for _____?
2.

Hiroko: Yes, and I'm making mushroom _____. I found the recipe
3.

in a magazine.

Martha: Will you serve your guests, or will they _____?
4.

Hiroko: I think I'll serve them.

Martha: Well, it sounds delicious. Your guests are going to _____!
5.

Did you buy special decorations?

Hiroko: I bought flowers for the table and _____ with pictures of
6.

turkeys on them.

Martha: Perfect!

UNIT 12 GRAMMAR EXERCISES

Grammar to Communicate 1:
Reflexive Pronouns

A Complete the conversations. Use the correct pronouns.

1. **A:** Do we have to wait for the hostess, or can we seat __ourselves__?

   B: You should wait for the hostess. She'll seat _____.

2. **A:** I don't want to go by _____. I don't like to eat alone.

   B: I haven't eaten yet. I'll go with _____.

3. **A:** Give _____ just a small piece. I'm not very hungry.

   B: That's because you stuffed _____ with candy before dinner!

4. **A:** Your son is really enjoying _____.

   B: Yes, he loves to play by _____.

5. **A:** It's my mother's birthday, so we're treating _____ to dinner.

   B: That's nice. Enjoy _____!

6. **A:** Are the kids hungry? I can make something for _____.

   B: Thanks, but they can make something for _____.

B Write ✓ if the underlined pronoun is correct. Write ✗ if it is incorrect. Then correct the incorrect pronouns.

___✓___ 1. My best friend and I have known <u>each other</u> since we were kids.

___✗___ 2. The waitress came when you were gone, so I ordered for <u>yourself</u>. *you*

_____ 3. He was hungry so he served <u>himself</u> more food.

_____ 4. You don't have to ask. You and your friends can help <u>yourself</u>.

_____ 5. In my culture, people do not talk to <u>each other</u> when they are eating.

_____ 6. I feel sorry for that woman. She always comes in alone and sits by <u>yourself</u>.

_____ 7. That man and his wife ate their dinner without speaking to <u>themselves</u>.

_____ 8. Oh my goodness! Is all of this food for <u>myself</u>?

Grammar to Communicate 2:
One / Ones

A   **Complete each sentence. Circle the letter of the correct answer.**

1. Do you want this dessert or that _____?

    (a.) one   **b.** ones

2. There are three glasses here. Which _____ is yours?

    a. one   **b.** ones

3. I don't need a napkin. I have _____.

    a. one   **b.** ones

4. I don't like this table. Can we have _____ over there, by the window?

    a. the one   **b.** the ones

5. These knives are dirty. Please bring us some clean _____.

    a. one   **b.** ones

6. All of the appetizers are delicious, but _____ with spinach are the best.

    a. the one   **b.** the ones

7. She's not our waitress. Our waitress is _____ with glasses.

    a. the one   **b.** the ones

B   **Match the questions with the answers. Write the correct letters.**

___f___ **1.** Are all the dishes good here?

_____ **2.** Do you like this restaurant?

_____ **3.** How about this table?

_____ **4.** Where's my napkin.

_____ **5.** Could I please have the pasta special?

_____ **6.** Do you want a cookie?

_____ **7.** Is that our waiter?

_____ **8.** Is this my pizza?

a. Well, that one by the window is nicer. . . .

b. Yes, but the one on Center St. is better.

c. I don't know. Ask the waitress for a new one.

d. Sorry, but we're out of that one.

e. Sure, I'll have one.

f. Yes, but ~~the ones with fish~~ are the best.

g. No, yours is the small one.

h. No, the one with the mustache is ours.

Grammar to Communicate 3:
Other: Singular and Plural

A   Look at the pictures. Complete the sentences. Use *another, the other,* or *the others*.

1.   There are several specials. One is tuna salad. ____*Another*____ is beef stew.

2.   There are two main dishes. _____ is pasta with vegetables. _____ is chicken.

3.   There are three kinds of ice cream in the ice cream sampler. One is vanilla. _____ are strawberry and chocolate.

4.   There are two desserts. One dessert costs $2.00. _____ costs $2.25.

5.   The hostess is seating two customers. _____ customer is serving herself from the salad bar.

6.   Two of the customers are female. _____ is male.

B   Put the conversation in the correct order. Write the correct numbers.

_____ One is lemon, another is chocolate, and the other is strawberry.

_____ I don't care. Surprise me!

__1__ What kind of cakes are those?

_____ Which one? The chocolate or the strawberry?

_____ Well, I like the lemon, but the others are good too.

_____ OK. I'll have two slices of the lemon. One for here and another to go.

_____ They all sound delicious. Which one do you recommend?

_____ So give me one of the others.

_____ I'm sorry, but there's only one slice of that one.

Review and Challenge

Complete the e-mail. Use the words in the box. (Be careful! There are extra words.)

another	me	ones	others	~~you~~
each other	myself	the one	themselves	yourself
himself	one	other	ourselves	yourselves

Ana,

How are you? I miss _____you_____! I can't believe that we haven't seen

_____ all summer! I hope you and Bob enjoyed _____ in Florida.
　　2.　　　　　　　　　　　　　　　　　　　　　　　　3.

We're fine. Jimmy spent a month with his cousins at my mother's house. They

really enjoyed _____. I was a little lonely, but it was good for Jimmy. He
　　　　　　　　4.

spends too much time by _____. He needs to be around _____
　　　　　　　　　　　　5.　　　　　　　　　　　　　　　　　　　6.

kids.

Anyway, Jimmy has _____ week of vacation before school starts.
　　　　　　　　　　7.

After that I'll have some free time. Would you like to meet for lunch? I'll

treat. There's a new Italian restaurant on Cypress St., next to that Mexican

_____. You know— _____ with the really good appetizers. Or if
　　8.　　　　　　　　　　　　9.

it's a nice day, we could meet in the park for a picnic. I'm tired of having lunch

by _____! Call me.
　　10.

Angela

UNIT 13 VOCABULARY EXERCISES

A   **Complete the story. Use the words in the box.**

burned CDs	downloaded	~~recorded~~
camcorder	installed	Web

Katie's boyfriend, Santos, plays guitar in a band called the Desperados. She uses technology to help his band. Last year, she ____recorded____ eight
1.
songs and _____ them onto her
2.
computer. Then she _____. She sold
3.
them at Desperados' concerts. Last week, she bought
a _____. She also _____ special
4.   5.
video software on her computer. Now she will be able to put videos on the
_____ for the Desperados' fans.
6.

B   **Complete the sentences. Use the words in the box.**

~~batteries~~	online	remote control
charge	operate	software

1. The radio isn't working. It needs new ____batteries____.

2. Our TV came with a _____, but we lost it.

3. I go _____ if I need help with my computer.

4. Ming's mother finds it hard to _____ her DVD player.

5. This _____ can help you pay your bills.

6. Did you remember to _____ the cell phone battery?

UNIT 13 GRAMMAR EXERCISES

Grammar to Communicate 1:
Can and *Be able to*

A   **Rewrite the sentences. Change *can* to *be able to* and *be able to* to *can*. Keep the same meaning.**

1. I can't access my e-mail from home.

    <u>I'm not able to access my e-mail from home.</u>

2. We are able to install any software.

    _____

3. He can't operate the remote control.

    _____

4. These days, people can make movies at home.

    _____

5. I can send e-mail, but I'm not able to open my messages.

    _____

6. I'm sorry, but we can't fix your DVD player.

    _____

B   **Complete the conversations. Use *have / has been able to* or *can*.**

1. **A:** We've been trying, but we <u>haven't been able to fix</u> your camera yet.
                                                    (fix)

    B: Give it to Tom. I think he _____<u>can fix</u>_____ it.
                                              (fix)

2. **A:** Something's wrong with my e-mail. I _____ it in a week.
                                                          (not, access)

    B: I'll call John. He _____ you.
                                      (help)

3. **A:** This computer _____ CDs, but it _____ them.
                                  (play)   (not burn)

    B: How about that one?

4. **A:** My daughter _____ a computer since she was 5.
                                  (operate)

    B: I know. My kids _____ anything on the computer.
                                    (do)

5. **A:** Computers _____ a lot of things better than people can.
                              (do)

    B: Yeah, but a computer _____ your friend.
                                          (not, be)

NAME: _____ DATE: _____

Grammar to Communicate 2:
Could and *Be able to*

A Rewrite the sentences. Change *could* to *was / were able to* and *was / were able to* to *could*. Keep the same meaning.

1. They couldn't access the Internet all day yesterday.

   They weren't able to access the Internet all day yesterday.

2. My great grandfather could fix any car.

   _____

3. We weren't able to charge the battery.

   _____

4. I wasn't able to find the website.

   _____

5. You could use a computer at 5 years old.

   _____

6. Before airplanes, most people weren't able to travel long distances.

   _____

B Complete the sentences. Use *was / were able to* and the verbs in the box. (Be careful! Some are affirmative, and some are negative.)

access	burn	~~charge~~	communicate	fix	install	record

1. I _*wasn't able to charge*_ your cell phone. You need a new battery.

2. We couldn't buy the ticket because we _____ the website.

3. She _____ the show. We can watch it later.

4. We _____ any CDs for you. Our CD burner is broken.

5. We _____ the computer. You don't need to buy a new one.

6. You bought the wrong software, so he _____ it.

7. When my husband was in Alaska, his cell phone didn't work, but we

   _____ by e-mail.

Grammar to Communicate 3:
Will be able to

A   **Write sentences about today and someday. Use *can* and *will be able to*.**

1. (live to 100)

   Today some people _____ *can live to 100* _____.

   Someday most people *will be able to live to 100* .

2. (have babies)

   Today women _____.

   Someday men _____.

3. (use a computer)

   Today many people _____.

   Someday everyone _____.

4. (walk on the moon /

   walk on Mars)

   Today we _____.

   Someday we _____.

5. (help people live longer /

   help people live forever)

   Today doctors _____.

   Someday doctors _____.

6. (travel to the moon /

   live on the moon)

   Today people _____.

   Someday people _____.

B   **Complete the conversations. Write questions with *will be able to*.**

1. **A:** I can't download the pictures onto this computer.

   B: _____ *Will you be able to download* _____ them onto my computer?

2. **A:** Customers can't order online yet.

   B: _____ online soon?

3. **A:** You can't use the computer now. I'm using it.

   B: _____ it later? _____

4. **A:** You can't use your cell phone. The battery needs to be charged.

   B: _____ it later?

5. **A:** They can't access the website today.

   B: _____ it tomorrow?

6. **A:** Right now hotel guests can't access the Internet from their rooms.

   B: When _____ it from their rooms?

Review and Challenge

Correct the letters. There are four mistakes in each letter. The first mistake is corrected for you.

Dear Doctor Al . . .

Dear Doctor Al,

Until last year, I ~~am~~ *was* able to work on the computer for ten hours a day with no problem.

Lately, however, I've been getting terrible headaches, and I have not been able to work for

more than an hour. Last week, I not able to finish an important project because I couldn't

use the computer. My boss is angry. I think I might lose my job. And if I am not able to

use a computer, I will never able to find another job. So far, no one is able to help me. You

are my last hope. Please help!

Sincerely,
Sick of the computer

Dear Sick of the Computer,

I'm surprised that your doctor couldn't able to help you. Your problem is very common,

and there are many things that you can to do. First of all, go to my website and you will

find links to some excellent eye doctors. Any one of them will be able to help you. But

here are some things you can do by yourself.

Make sure that you able to look straight at the middle of your computer screen without

moving your head up or down. If you need to move your head, change the position of

your chair or your computer. And when you are working on the computer, take a short

break every 15 minutes. If you couldn't get up and move around, just look away from the

computer screen. If you do these two simple things, I think your headaches will go away.

Good luck!
Doctor Al

UNIT 14 VOCABULARY EXERCISES

A   Read the rules for children at Olympia Summer Camp. Complete the
sentences. Use the words in the box.

| apologize | ~~behave~~ | hold | obey | take out the trash |

RULES FOR OLYMPIA CAMPERS

1. Children must ___behave___ well at all times.

2. When children work in the kitchen, they must _____.

3. Older children must _____ the hands of younger children on walks.

4. Any child who hurts another child must _____ to him or her.

5. If children do not _____ these rules, they will go home early!

B   Complete the sentences. Use the words in the box.

| bothers | crosses | ~~do chores~~ | punishes | strict |

1. Alan has to ___do chores___ with his family every Saturday.

2. Hee Jung's mother _____ her if she doesn't finish her homework.

3. When I was a teenager, my parents were _____. I had to come

home by 9:00 on Saturday night.

4. May is very careful when she _____ the street.

5. Elena's brother pulls her hair. This _____ her.

NAME: _____   DATE: _____

UNIT 14 GRAMMAR EXERCISES

Grammar to Communicate 1:
Have to / *Have got to* / *Must*: **Affirmative Statements**
Have to: *Yes* / *No* **Questions**

A   **Look at the pictures. Answer the questions. Write long answers.**

1. Do Henry and Claire Morgan have to go to bed?
   ___No. They've got to OR They have to___ do chores.

2. Does Henry have to do the dishes?
   _____ take out the trash.

3. Does Claire have to take out the trash?
   _____ do the dishes.

4. Do the children have to watch TV?
   _____ turn off the TV.

5. Do they have to fight?
   _____ behave well.

6. Do they have to punish their mother?
   _____ obey their mother.

B   **Write questions. Put the words in the correct order.**

1. _Do the kids have to go to bed early every night?_
   (the kids / go to bed / every night / have to / do / early)

2. _____
   (have to / any chores / does / do / your little boy)

3. _____
   (obey / have to / I / do / her)

4. _____
   (I / do / finish / have to / my vegetables)

5. _____
   (today / do / the kids / go to school / have to)

6. _____
   (take / does / your daughter / classes / have to / this summer)

Grammar to Communicate 2:
Does not have to and *Must not*

A **Match the beginnings of the sentences to their endings. Write the correct letters.**

___c___ 1. You don't have to play with Jen,   **a.** but your clothes must be neat.

_____ 2. You don't have to talk in class,   **b.** but you must be on time.

_____ 3. You don't have to arrive early,   **c.** ~~but you mustn't fight with her.~~

_____ 4. You don't have to wear a uniform,   **d.** but you mustn't walk alone.

_____ 5. You don't have to clean the house,   **e.** but you mustn't make a mess.

_____ 6. You don't have to walk with us,   **f.** but you must do homework.

B **Complete the conversations. Use *don't / doesn't have to* or *mustn't*.**

1. **A:** You _____*mustn't*_____ leave the children alone in the car.

   B: Don't worry, I won't.

2. **A:** We _____ forget to pick the kids up after school.

   B: I know.

3. **A:** You _____ hit your little sister.

   B: But Mom, she took my ball.

4. **A:** Why isn't Jack helping me with the dishes?

   B: It's his birthday. He _____ do any chores today.

5. **A:** It's the first day of school. You _____ be late.

   B: I won't be. I'm leaving right now.

6. **A:** The children _____ go to school tomorrow. It's a holiday.

   B: Great! We can go to the zoo.

7. **A:** The students at this school _____ wear uniforms.

   B: Can they wear jeans and sneakers?

NAME: _____   DATE: _____

Grammar to Communicate 3:
Had to: Statements and Questions

A **Complete the sentences about Molly's life. Use *had to* or *didn't have to*.**

1. When Molly was three, her mother ___had to go___ back to work.
(go)
2. She _____ Molly in daycare.
(put)
3. Molly was the only child. She _____ her bedroom.
(share)
4. Molly's sister, Lisa, was born when she was 10. Molly _____ her a lot.
(babysit)
5. Lisa _____ any chores. Molly did everything.
(do)
6. Molly wanted to go to a good college, so she _____ a lot in high school.
(study)
7. After she started studying a lot, she _____ her sister anymore.
(take care of)

B **Jane is asking Molly about when she was a high school student. Complete their conversation. Read Molly's answers. Then write questions.**

Jane: What kind of uniform ___did you have to wear___ to school?
1.

Molly: We didn't have to wear uniforms. We wore our own clothes.

Jane: How often _____ to school?
2.

Molly: We never had to walk to school. We took the bus.

Jane: How much _____ for your books?
3.

Molly: Our parents didn't have to pay anything. The books were free.

Jane: How often _____ the classroom?
4.

Molly: The students never had to clean the classroom. The janitors did it.

Jane: How many days a week _____ to school?
5.

Molly: We had to go to school six days a week—Monday through Saturday.

Jane: Who _____ a desk with?
6.

Molly: We didn't have to share our desks. We had our own desks.

NAME: _____   DATE: _____

Review and Challenge

Find the mistake in each conversation. Circle the letter and correct the mistake.

1. **A:** Why <u>do</u> we <u>have to</u> get up so early?   **Correct:** _got to go_
            A   B

    B: Because <u>you've</u> <u>got go</u> to school.
            C   (D)

2. **A:** <u>Do</u> I <u>have</u> <u>to obey</u> her?   **Correct:** _____
         A   B   C

    B: Of course you <u>have</u>! She's your grandmother.
                   D

3. **A:** <u>How much</u> <u>does</u> he have to pay for the bus?   **Correct:** _____
           A   B

    B: He's only five. He <u>mustn't</u> <u>pay</u> anything.
                C   D

4. **A:** <u>Do</u> I have <u>to hold</u> your hand?   **Correct:** _____
         A   B

    B: No, but you <u>must</u> <u>to stay</u> next to me.
             C   D

5. **A:** Why does he <u>has</u> <u>to come</u> with us?   **Correct:** _____
               A   B

    B: Because I <u>have</u> <u>to go</u> to work.
             C D

6. **A:** Why <u>didn't</u> <u>you</u> come last night?   **Correct:** _____
            A B

    B: I <u>must</u> <u>babysit</u> for my little sister.
          C   D

7. **A:** The kids <u>hadn't</u> <u>to go</u> to school because of the snow.   **Correct:** _____
              A   B

    B: Really? The high school was open. My kids <u>had</u> <u>to go</u>.
                          C   D

8. **A:** It's Monday. <u>Why</u> <u>are you</u> at home?   **Correct:** _____
                  A   B

    B: My son's sick, so I <u>had</u> <u>to taking</u> the day off.
                     C   D

9. **A:** In my culture, children <u>don't have to</u> <u>talk</u> during meals.   **Correct:** _____
                       A   B

    B: Really? <u>Do</u> they <u>have to be</u> quiet all the time?
               C   D

10. **A:** <u>Had you</u> <u>to go</u> to school yesterday?   **Correct:** _____
           A   B

    B: No. We never <u>have to</u> <u>go</u> to school on Sunday.
                  C   D

UNIT 15 VOCABULARY EXERCISE

Sun's friend Kelly has bad manners. Complete the sentences about Kelly. Use the words in the box.

cover her mouth	puts her elbows
interrupts	talk about people behind their backs
~~knock on the door~~	talks with her mouth full
licks	whisper

1. Kelly doesn't ___*knock on the door*___ before she enters a room.

2. At dinner, Kelly _____ on the table.

3. When Sun is talking, Kelly _____ her.

4. You shouldn't _____. But Kelly tells terrible stories about her friends.

5. Kelly coughs a lot, but she doesn't _____.

6. Kelly doesn't use a napkin at dinner—she _____ her fingers.

7. When Kelly eats, she takes big bites and _____. Sun can't understand what Kelly is saying.

8. At the library, people should _____, but Kelly always talks loudly.

UNIT 15 GRAMMAR EXERCISES

Grammar to Communicate 1:
Should (not) + Verb

 A   Look at the pictures. Complete the sentences. Use *should* or *shouldn't*.

1.

He ___should___ cover his mouth.

3.

She _____ lick her fingers.

5.

She _____ interrupt her mother.

2.

He _____ knock on the door.

4.

They _____ talk about her behind her back.

6.

She _____ talk with her mouth full.

B   Jin is going to a dinner party. She's asking her mother what she should do. Complete Jin's questions. Use *should* and the words in the box.

bring for the hostess	put my hands	sit	take	talk to

1. **A:** What should I bring for the hostess?

    B: Some flowers or a box of chocolates.

2. **A:** Where _____

    B: Your hostess will tell you where to sit.

3. **A:** Where _____

    B: In your lap.

4. **A:** Who _____

    B: The person sitting next to you.

5. **A:** How much food _____

    B: A little bit of everything.

Grammar to Communicate 2:
Should (not) + *Be* + Present Participle

A   What should the people be doing? Complete the sentences. Use *should be* and a verb in the box.

carry	listen	~~stand~~	use a napkin	whisper	work

1. Why are you sitting? You ___*should be standing*___ .

2. Why are they talking so loud? They _____ .

3. Why are you licking your fingers? You _____ .

4. Why are you carrying that? Your son _____ it.

5. Why are you talking? You _____ .

6. Why is she staring out the window? She _____ .

B   Read each situation. Write a sentence with *should* and one with *shouldn't*.

1. Jerry isn't listening to his teacher. He's talking to his friend.

   He should be listening to his teacher. He shouldn't be talking to his friend.

2. Amy isn't eating her vegetables. She's feeding them to the dog.

   _____

   _____

3. You're drinking milk from the carton. You aren't using a glass.

   _____

   _____

4. Liz isn't serving her guests. She's serving herself.

   _____

   _____

5. The boys are getting on the bus. They're not waiting for others to get off first.

   _____

   _____

Grammar to Communicate 3:
Should and *Have to*

A   **Complete each sentence. Circle the letter of the correct answer.**

1. He's a waiter. He _____ serve customers.

   a. should   **ⓑ. has to**   c. doesn't have to

2. She's a waitress. She _____ be rude to the customers.

   a. shouldn't   b. doesn't have to   c. don't have to

3. He's the dishwasher. He _____ wash dishes.

   a. should   b. shouldn't   c. has to

4. They're chauffeurs. They _____ have drivers licenses.

   a. should   b. has to   c. have to

5. We're classmates. We _____ be friends.

   a. should   b. has to   c. have to

6. You're the hostess. You _____ seat the customers.

   a. should   b. have to   c. don't have to

7. We're cooks. We _____ meet the customers.

   a. should   b. have to   c. don't have to

B   **Complete the sentences. Use *should, shouldn't, have / has to*, or *don't / doesn't have to*.**

1. Cashiers _____*have to*_____ be able to use a cash register, but they
   _____*don't have to*_____ be able to fix it.

2. Customers _____ wash their hands before they eat.

   Cooks _____ wash their hands before they cook.

3. In a hotel, the housekeepers _____ clean the rooms.

   They _____ talk to the guests.

4. Hotel guests _____ clean their own rooms, but they

   _____ make a mess.

5. At a self-serve gas station, the customers _____

   pump their own gas. At a full-serve gas station, the attendants

   _____ pump the customers' gas.

6. Coworkers _____ be friends, but they

   _____ be rude to one another.

Review and Challenge

Correct the conversation. There are eight mistakes. The first mistake is corrected for you.

Ray: What are you doing in the kitchen? You should be ~~spend~~ *spending* time with your

guests.

Shana: But I have to cook.

Ray: Well, the guests look very uncomfortable.

Shana: Well, what do I have to do? Someone have to finish cooking the dinner.

Ray: You should go out there and talk to your guests. And you should leave them

alone again. I'll finish in here.

Shana: Thanks, but you aren't have to do that. You're busy, and they're my guests.

Ray: You're right. I haven't to help you. But I want to.

Shana: But you should studying for your exams.

Ray: I've finished studying. Now tell me, what should I have to do?

Shana: Well, the meat has to cook for 30 minutes, but you have to turn it over after

20 minutes. It has to cook on both sides.

Ray: That's it?

Shana: Yes. Everything else is ready.

UNIT 16 VOCABULARY EXERCISES

 A   Look at the picture. Complete the sentences. Use the words in the box.

~~barking~~	driveway	garden	slamming the door

1. The dog must be _____barking_____ at the man.

2. The kids are running out of the house. They are _____.

3. The Montoyas must be visiting their grandchildren. That's their trailer in the

    _____.

4. This is a beautiful _____. The woman must like plants.

B **Complete the e-mail message. Use the words in the box.**

| chat | gardeners | junk | musician | shouting | ~~yard~~ |

From: Daniela Cook

To: Francoise Goulet

Subject: Our new house

Hi Francoise!

We love our new neighborhood. We have a big ___yard___
1.
filled with flowers. The previous owners must have been good

_____. Our neighbors are nice, but they're a little
2.
strange. They have a lot of _____ in their yard.
3.
They're loud too! They're always _____. Their son
4.
plays his guitar all the time. He's pretty good, so he must be a

_____. Our neighbors are loud, but they're nice.
5.
They always want to _____ with us. And they gave us
6.
a pie yesterday!

Your friend,

Daniela

UNIT 16 GRAMMAR EXERCISES

Grammar to Communicate 1:
Must + Verb

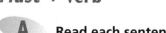 **A** **Read each sentence. Circle the letter of the correct response.**

1. They leave their dog alone all day.

   a. The dog must be old.   **b.** The dog must be lonely.

2. I haven't seen Robert in a few days.

   a. He must be on a business trip.   **b.** He must be retired.

3. I saw our new neighbor at the supermarket. She was buying diapers.

   a. She must like children.   **b.** She must have a baby.

4. Nobody visits Mrs. Jones.

   a. She must be a widow.   **b.** She must be bored.

5. Jimmy Kelly hasn't been in school for a couple of days.

   a. He must be sick.   **b.** He must have a new teacher.

6. Sid has been walking to work lately.

   a. He must need the exercise.   **b.** He must be fat.

B **Write sentences about the Robinsons and the Ramseys. Use *must* and the words in the box.**

be old	have a gardener	live far away
be retired	have good jobs	~~work~~

1. The Robbs are never home during the day. _____ *They must work.* _____

2. They have a very big house. _____

3. Their garden is beautiful. _____

4. The Ramseys' son is 55. _____

5. They are home all day. _____

6. Their children visit them once a year. _____

Grammar to Communicate 2:
Must + *Be* + Present Participle

A Match the facts with the logical conclusions. Write the correct letters.

___f__ **1.** She's all wet.

_____ **2.** She's carrying her briefcase.

_____ **3.** There are about twenty kids in their backyard.

_____ **4.** He was smiling yesterday.

_____ **5.** She left the house in sneakers.

_____ **6.** They just left with suitcases.

_____ **7.** He just shouted at her.

a. They must be having a party.

b. He must be feeling better.

c. They must be fighting.

d. She must be going to work.

e. They must be going on vacation.

f. It must be raining.

g. She must be going to the gym.

B Complete the conversations. Use *must* and the words in the box.

babysit	move	~~visit~~	work
date	practice	walk	

1. **A:** Whose car is that in the Trents' driveway?

   B: It must be their daughter's. She ___must be visiting___.

2. **A:** Who's that girl next door with Billy Anderson?

   B: That's his old girlfriend. They _____ again.

3. **A:** Who are those little kids over at Mrs. Johnson's place?

   B: They must be her grandchildren. She _____ them.

4. **A:** Why is there a moving van next door?

   B: The new owners _____ in.

5. **A:** Why aren't the Amores answering their phone?

   B: It's Monday morning. They _____.

6. **A:** Where is that music coming from?

   B: Doris _____ for the concert.

7. **A:** Why is Fluffy barking?

   B: Someone _____ in front of the house.

Grammar to Communicate 3:
Must not and *Can't*

A   Write ✓ if the underlined part of the sentence is correct. Write ✗ if it is incorrect. Then correct the incorrect sentences.

   ✓ 1. **A:** Jen just pulled up in front of the house.   ― ― ―

          B: That can't be Jen. I just talked to her <u>at work</u>.

   ✗ 2. **A:** The neighbor's dog is barking.   *don't have*

          B: That can't be their dog. They <u>have</u> a dog.

   ____ 3. **A:** Your cell phone is ringing.   _____

          B: That can't be mine. I <u>lost</u> my cell phone.

   ____ 4. **A:** I <u>haven't</u> seen Tina and Bob together lately.   _____

          B: They must not be going out any more.

   ____ 5. **A:** Terry was <u>in a good mood</u> this morning.   _____

          B: She and her husband must not be getting along.

B   Complete the conversations. Use *can't* or *must not*.

   1. **A:** That must be the neighbor's cat.

       B: It ___*can't*___ be their cat. This one's black, and theirs is white.

   2. **A:** Our new neighbor has three kids.

       B: Are you kidding? She _____ have three kids! She's too young.

   3. **A:** I think Mr. Parks is out gardening.

       B: Mr. Parks _____ be out gardening! He's too sick.

   4. **A:** Where's the moving truck? I thought they were leaving today.

       B: I thought so too, but they _____ be moving until tomorrow.

   5. **A:** Are Sue and Betsy best friends?

       B: They _____ be best friends. They don't spend very much time together.

Review and Challenge

Correct the conversation. There are seven mistakes. The first mistake is corrected for you.

Mary: I can't wait to hear about the Cohen's trip! I think I'll go over there.

Steve: I don't think that's a good idea. They got in really late last night. They ~~mustn't~~ *must* be sleeping.

Mary: Are you kidding? They can't be sleep! It's 11:00. They always get up early.

Steve: Yeah, but they didn't get home until 3:00 A.M. They can be tired.

Mary: Well one of them must being awake. I can see lights over there. I'm going over.

Mary: Yoo hoo, Sal? Ethel? Are you there?

Sal: Mary! Is that you?

Mary: Yes. Welcome home! How was your trip? You must be having a million photos. Where's Ethel?

Sal: She's sleeping.

Mary: Oh, I'm so sorry.

Sal: That's OK. Come on in. But I don't have any photos to show you.

Mary: Oh, come on! You can be serious. You always take photos.

Sal: Well, not this time. I didn't even take my camera.

Mary: You must be joke.

Sal: You're right, I am joking. You know me too well, Mary. Anyway, have a seat and I'll make us some coffee. Then I'll show you the pictures.

UNIT 17 VOCABULARY EXERCISES

A Complete the conversation. Use the words in the box.

common	~~gained~~	get in shape	high cholesterol	vitamin C

Doctor Bellini: Good morning, George. Why are you here today?

George: I've _____*gained*_____ ten pounds this year. I feel unhealthy.

1.

Doctor Bellini: That's _____ for men your age.

2.

Do you eat healthy meals?

George: No. I'm too busy to eat well.

Doctor Bellini: You need to eat better. It's a good idea to eat foods

that have _____, like oranges

3.

and tomatoes. Do you get enough exercise?

George: I exercise once a week.

Doctor Bellini: You need to exercise three times a week to

_____.

4.

George: Should I worry about _____, too?

5.

Doctor Bellini: Yes, and it's important to check that once a year. We'll check it today.

B Complete the sentences. Use the words in the box.

blood pressure	calcium	~~get shots~~	have surgery	weak

1. Children need to _____*get shots*_____ every year to protect them from the flu.

2. Betsy forgot to eat all day. In the evening, she felt _____.

3. It is important to take _____ pills for strong bones.

4. Some people who have high _____ need to take medicine to

lower it.

5. Mr. Lee has a serious heart problem. He needs to _____.

UNIT 17 GRAMMAR EXERCISES

Grammar to Communicate 1:
It + Infinitive

A Write sentences. Use *It* + infinitive.

1. It is important for teenagers to get 8 hours of sleep a night.
    (important / teenagers /get 8 hours of sleep)

2. _____
    (necessary / toddlers / take a nap every day)

3. _____
    (not normal / teenagers / sleep all day)

4. _____
    (normal / infants/ sleep most of the day)

5. _____
    (common / middle-aged people/ gain weight)

6. _____
    (a good idea / children over three / visit the dentist twice a year)

B Rewrite the sentences. Keep the same meaning. Use *for* where necessary.

1. Patients on this medicine usually gain weight.
    It is common _for patients on this medicine to gain weight_ .

2. Most people feel weak after surgery.
    It is normal _____ to feel weak after surgery _____ .

3. Pregnant women often get morning sickness.
    It is normal _____ .

4. Healthy adults need to have a cholesterol test every five years.
    It is necessary _____ .

5. Most people don't have a lot of pain after this kind of surgery.
    It isn't normal _____ .

6. People need to exercise every day.
    It is a good idea _____ .

7. You have to lose weight.
    It is important _____ .

Grammar to Communicate 2:
Too and *Enough* + Infinitive

A **Match the beginnings of the sentences to their endings. Write the correct letters.**

_c_ **1.** The doctor is too busy   **a.** to stop the pain.

_____ **2.** He isn't sick enough   **b.** for two patients to stay in.

_____ **3.** This medicine isn't strong enough   **c.** to take any new patients.

_____ **4.** You're not old enough   **d.** for you to eat.

_____ **5.** The room is too small   **e.** to take care of yourself.

_____ **6.** That meal is too unhealthy   **f.** to take to the hospital.

_____ **7.** This pill is too big   **g.** for a child to take.

B **Complete the sentences. Use *too*, *very*, or *enough*.**

1. I need to take a nap. I'm _____too tired_____ to drive.
                                    (tired)

2. It's _____ to go outside. Our coats aren't
              (cold)

_____.
      (warm)

3. You're _____ to be on a diet! You should be gaining
                (thin)
weight, not losing it.

4. It's going to be _____ tomorrow. A perfect day for the
                        (hot)
beach!

5. I'm calling the doctor. Your fever is _____. It isn't
                                            (high)
normal.

6. You need to wait another year. You aren't _____ to have
                                                  (old)
the surgery.

7. The doctor is _____, but if you can wait, he'll talk to
                      (busy)
you as soon as he can.

NAME: _____   DATE: _____

Grammar to Communicate 3:
Infinitives of Purpose

 A   **Complete the conversations. Use the words in the box.**

to buy some cold medicine	to get in shape	to prevent a cold	to stop a headache
to get a cleaning	~~to hear better~~	to see better	

1. **A:** What can you do _____to hear better_____?   **B:** Wear a hearing aid.

2. **A:** What can you do _____?   **B:** Wear glasses.

3. **A:** Who should you call _____?   **B:** A dentist.

4. **A:** Where can you go _____?   **B:** A pharmacy.

5. **A:** What can you do _____?   **B:** Exercise.

6. **A:** What should you take _____?   **B:** Vitamin C.

7. **A:** What can you do _____?   **B:** Take an aspirin.

B   **Rewrite the sentences. Use *to* + verb.**

1. He's taking medication because he needs to gain weight.

   He's taking medication to gain weight. _____

2. She's studying to be a doctor because she wants to help people.

   _____

3. I'm on a diet because I have to lose weight.

   _____

4. He washes his hands several times a day because he wants to stay healthy.

   _____

5. He is having knee surgery because he wants to be able to run.

   _____

6. I put a bandage on the cut because I wanted to keep it clean.

   _____

7. She is resting a lot because she needs to get stronger.

   _____

Review and Challenge

Find the mistake in each item. Circle the letter and correct the mistake.

1. It isn't <u>necessary</u> <u>for you</u> to stay in the hospital. You aren't <u>enough sick</u> <u>to be</u> here.
   A   B   Ⓒ   D

   Correct: <u>sick enough</u>

2. <u>It's</u> not a good idea <u>to him</u> to <u>travel</u> right now. His blood pressure is <u>too high</u>.
   A   B   C   D

   Correct: _____

3. People come here <u>to rest</u>. It's <u>too quiet</u>, so it's <u>easy</u> <u>to relax</u>.
                     A   B   C   D

   Correct: _____

4. He <u>must eat</u> <u>to get</u> stronger. It will be impossible <u>for</u> operate if he's <u>too weak</u>.
      A   B   C   D

   Correct: _____

5. She <u>isn't able</u> <u>to take</u> care of herself anymore, and we are <u>very busy</u> <u>to help</u> her.
       A   B   C   D

   Correct: _____

6. You <u>aren't getting</u> <u>enough</u> exercise to <u>losing weight</u>. Your cholesterol is <u>too high</u>.
      A   B   C   D

   Correct: _____

7. He is <u>very sick</u> <u>to have</u> visitors. Anyway, <u>it's</u> <u>too late</u>. Visiting hours end at 9:00.
        A   B   C   D

   Correct: _____

8. It was <u>too noisy</u> <u>for me</u> to sleep in the hospital. I needed <u>to come</u> home <u>for resting</u>.
         A   B   C   D

   Correct: _____

9. You need <u>stronger medicine</u> <u>to stop</u> the pain. That medicine <u>is</u> <u>strong enough</u>.
           A   B   C   D

   Correct: _____

10. <u>It is</u> necessary <u>all employees</u> <u>to know</u> CPR. You need to take a course <u>to work</u> here.
    A   B   C   D

    Correct: _____

UNIT 18 VOCABULARY EXERCISES

A   **Complete the conversation. Use the words in the box.**

~~'m bad at~~	am tired of	dislikes	is into	prefers	sewing

Orham: Excuse me. I need help buying a birthday present for my sister.

I <u>'m bad at</u> _____ shopping. It's difficult for me.
　　　　　　　　1.

Salesperson: Does your sister like music? We have CDs. Does she like country music?

Orham: No, she doesn't. She _____ pop music. But she has a
　　　　　　　　　　　　　　　　　2.

lot of CDs.

Salesperson: What does she like to do?

Orham: She _____ making her own clothes. She does it all
　　　　　　　　　　　3.

the time.

Salesperson: I have an idea. We just got a new book about _____.
　　　　　　　　　　　　　　　　　　　　　　　　　　　　　　4.

Orham: She _____ learning from books. She thinks it's easier
　　　　　　　　　5.

to learn from a DVD. Do you have any DVDs?

Salesperson: Yes, the author of that book also has a DVD.

Orham: I think my sister would like that! Besides, I _____
　　　　　　　　　　　　　　　　　　　　　　　　　　　　6.

shopping. I've been here since early this morning.

B   **Complete the sentences. Use the words in the box.**

camping	consider	is good at
can't stand	hike	knitting

1. Sita loves _____camping_____, but her husband doesn't. He prefers to sleep in a hotel.

2. Mike _____ computer games. He has the highest score for Space Raiders.

3. When you _____ in the mountains, you need good shoes.

4. Michael is _____ a sweater for his wife.

5. Sally wants to be an artist. She should _____ taking a painting class.

6. Yuri _____ root beer. He thinks it tastes like medicine.

UNIT 18 GRAMMAR EXERCISES

Grammar to Communicate 1:
Gerunds as Subjects

A Complete the sentences. Use the gerund form of the verbs in the box.

be	camp	knit	play	~~ride~~	spend	take

1. _____Riding_____ horses can be expensive.

2. _____ games is good for children.

3. _____ a sweater takes a long time.

4. _____ lessons is the best way to learn to play an instrument.

5. _____ alone can be dangerous.

6. _____ time with your family is good for your health.

7. _____ a musician is fun, but it isn't easy.

B Rewrite the sentences. Begin each sentence with a gerund. Keep the same meaning.

1. It's easy to ride a bike.

   Riding a bike isn't difficult. _____
   (difficult)

2. It isn't good for kids to watch too much TV.

   _____
   (bad)

3. It's not safe to ride a bike without a helmet.

   _____
   (dangerous)

4. It's expensive to take care of a horse.

   _____
   (cheap)

5. It's a bad idea to swim alone.

   _____
   (good idea)

6. It's not fun to go to the mall.

   _____
   (boring)

Grammar to Communicate 2:
Gerunds as Objects of Prepositions

A   Complete the sentences. Use the words in the box.

at playing	into camping	of getting	to being
~~in taking~~	like going	on studying	up knitting

1. We're interested _____ in taking _____ drawing lessons.

2. I don't feel _____ to work today. I'm tired.

3. She won't join the team. She's scared _____ hurt.

4. I'm not _____. Sleeping outside is not fun.

5. Summer is coming. I'm looking forward _____ able to eat outside.

6. If you want to be good _____ an instrument, you have to practice a lot.

7. I've taken _____. My grandmother is teaching me.

8. They're playing too much. They're not concentrating _____.

B   Write sentences. Use a preposition and a gerund.

1. I'm scared of swimming in deep water. _____

(I'm scared / swim in deep water)

2. _____

(many children dream / become famous)

3. _____

(we are looking forward / go on vacation)

4. _____

(please think / join the team)

5. _____

(he's good / do things with his hands)

6. _____

(they are concentrating / learn to cook)

7. _____

(we're excited / win the game)

NAME: _____   DATE: _____

Grammar to Communicate 3:
Gerunds or Infinitives as Objects of Verbs

A Write ✓ if the sentence is correct. Write ✗ if it is incorrect. Then correct the incorrect sentences.

   _✓_ 1. He enjoys ~~to play~~ *playing* computer games.

   _✗_ 2. She loves to play computer games.

   _____ 3. I can't stand practicing the piano.

   _____ 4. We expect winning the game.

   _____ 5. I miss playing tennis.

   _____ 6. He prefers to listen to music.

   _____ 7. I stopped to dance when I hurt my leg.

   _____ 8. She dislikes to fish.

B Rewrite the sentences. Keep the same meaning.

1. They're into cooking. _They enjoy cooking._ (enjoy)

2. They don't like to bake. _____ (dislike)

3. I'm going to give up running. _____ (stop)

4. We are taking up painting. _____ (learn)

5. Do you feel like dancing? _____ (want)

6. She's thinking about taking guitar lessons. _____ (consider)

7. Of course we would like to win. _____ (hope)

Center Stage 3, Unit 18 Grammar Exercises 97

NAME: _____   DATE: _____

Review and Challenge

Complete the letter. Use the words in the box. (Be careful! There are extra words.)

to ask	to have	~~living~~	to see	surprising
to be	having	to lose	seeing	to swim
being	to live	losing	to surprise	swimming

Dear Josie,

How are you? Things are going pretty well, but ___living___ alone here isn't
                                                      1.
easy. I miss _____ all of you every day. And every night I go to bed and
              2.
dream of _____ a big plate of mom's chicken and rice!
           3.
Guess what? I've taken up _____! I've joined a health club, and I
                            4.
go there _____ every day. And I have some other big news. I've decided
          5.
_____ Marisa to marry me. I'm worried about _____ her to some
  6.   7.
other guy. And anyway, _____ single isn't as much fun as it used to be. I
                         8.
hope _____ enough money for a ring soon. But please don't say anything. I
      9.
want _____ her.
      10.
Well, that's all my news. Write back soon with the news from home!

Love,

Alex

UNIT 19 VOCABULARY EXERCISES

A   Complete the news story about a fire. Use the words in the box.

advised	fire hazards	~~smoke detectors~~
ambulance	paramedics	suspects

Fire at Luxor Apartments

Grover City. Last night, there was a fire at the Luxor apartment building on Baker Street. The fire burned for several hours, and it damaged many of the apartments in the building. Luckily, no people were hurt, because the ___smoke detectors___
1.
in the apartments were working. All the residents must have heard them, because they all got out of the building. However, several people felt sick from the smoke, so firefighters called an _____. The _____
2.   3.
took the sick people to the hospital.

Fire Chief Michael Torres _____ that a candle in
4.
an apartment on the fifth floor started the fire. He _____
5.
everybody to get rid of their candles because they are _____.
6.

B Complete the news story about a robbery. Use the words in the box.

encouraged	notice	speeding
guess	~~ordering~~	ticket

First Federal Bank Robbers Caught

Springfield. At 11:15 this morning, three men entered the First Federal Savings

Bank and started _____ordering_____ the workers to give them all the money.

1.

At first the bank manager didn't _____ the men's guns. The

2.

manager _____ his employees to stay calm.

3.

The police asked employees to _____ how much money

4.

was stolen. They thought it was at least $20,000. Unfortunately, no one could

describe the robbers. However, 30 minutes later, police stopped a car outside

of Springfield for _____. The police officer was writing the

5.

_____ when he saw bags of money in the backseat!

6.

UNIT 19 GRAMMAR EXERCISES

Grammar to Communicate 1:
Verb + Object + Infinitive

A Complete the paragraph about Mr. Matthews and his daughter. Use *he, she, her* or *him*.

Mr. Matthews is a firefighter. _____He_____ encouraged his daughter to
                                      1.

take the test to become a firefighter too. At first _____ wasn't sure,
                                                          2.

but _____ convinced _____ to take it. _____ asked
         3.   4.   5.

_____ to help her with the test. _____ advised _____ to get
      6.   7.   8.

into shape. _____ wanted _____ to pass the test. She worked very
                 9.   10.

hard. _____ expected _____ to do well, and she did. Now she's a
           11.   12.

firefighter, just like her father.

B Write sentences. Put the words in the correct order.

1. The police officer warned the tenants to lock their windows.
    <u>(their windows / the police officer / the tenants / to lock / warned)</u>

2. _____
    (the landlord / the fire inspector / the problem / advised / to fix)

3. _____
    (ordered / to leave / the firefighters / the tenants / the building)

4. _____
    (the police officer / doesn't want / Ana / a ticket / her / to give)

5. _____
    (to go / the paramedics / the old woman / to the hospital / convinced)

6. _____
    (to the hospital / needs / to take / the injured woman / her / an ambulance)

7. _____
    (her / allowed / to help / she / the paramedics)

Grammar to Communicate 2:
Verb + Noun Clause and Replacing Noun Clauses

A   **Combine the sentences. Use a noun clause.**

1. The neighborhood is dangerous. The police know this.

   The police know (that) the neighborhood is dangerous.

2. There aren't enough police officers. Everyone thinks this.

   _____

3. They need the help of the people in the community. The police believe this.

   _____

4. The police don't care about them. The people in the neighborhood suspect this.

   _____

5. The neighborhood's people want to help them. The police don't believe this.

   _____

6. The neighborhood will be safe in the future. Everyone hopes this.

   _____

B   **Complete the conversations. Use *so* or *not*.**

1. **A:** Is the landlord going to install new smoke detectors?

   B: I don't know, but I _____ hope so _____.
                                   (hope)

2. **A:** Is he a paramedic?

   B: I _____. He drives an ambulance.
              (guess)

3. **A:** Are you sure that he's a police officer?

   B: I _____. He has a badge.
              (think)

4. **A:** Is he a paramedic? He doesn't know how to do CPR.

   B: Then I _____.
                  (guess)

5. **A:** Is she going to die?

   B: I _____. She's doing much better today.
              (think)

6. **A:** Was anyone hurt in the fire?

   B: I _____. It wasn't a very serious fire.
              (believe)

Grammar to Communicate 3:
Make and Let

A   Complete the sentences. Use *let*, *made*, *didn't let*, or *didn't make*.

1. The police officer _____*made*_____ me stop because I was speeding.

2. The firefighters _____ us use the elevators.

3. The boy was happy. The policeman _____ him see his badge.

4. I convinced them that I wasn't hurt, so they _____ me go to the hospital.

5. The man was speeding, so the police _____ him stop his car.

6. The fire inspector _____ the landlord fix the smoke detectors.

B   Complete the sentences. Use *make* or *let*. Be careful! Some sentences are negative.

1. The police officer didn't make us stay. He _____*let us go*_____.

2. The firefighters made the guests go outside. They _____.

(let, stay inside)

3. The paramedics allowed me to ride in the ambulance. They

   _____.
   (make, get out)

4. The fire inspector didn't permit them to open the restaurant. She

   _____.
   (let, open)

5. The police officer ordered him to get out of the car. He _____.
   (make, get out)

6. The firefighters permitted the employees to take the elevator. They

   _____.
   (let, take the elevator)

Review and Challenge

Find the mistake in each conversation. Circle the letter and correct the mistake.

1. **A:** Did they <u>let the mother</u> <u>to ride</u> in the ambulance?
                       A   (B)
           Correct: _____ride_____

   B: I <u>don't know</u>, but I <u>hope so</u>.
          C   D

2. **A:** What did the police officer <u>advise you</u> <u>to do</u>?
                           A   B
           Correct: _____

   B: He <u>told you</u> <u>to hire</u> a lawyer.
           C   D

3. **A:** <u>Have the firefighters</u> <u>let the workers</u> <u>return</u> to their offices?
             A   B   C
           Correct: _____

   B: No, I <u>don't think that</u>.
               D

4. **A:** Did the paramedics <u>encourage her</u> <u>to call</u> the police?
                    A   B
           Correct: _____

   B: Yes, but she didn't. I think <u>why</u> <u>she was scared</u>.
                          C   D

5. **A:** <u>Do you expect</u> them <u>to reopen</u> the restaurant soon?
          A   B
           Correct: _____

   B: <u>No, I don't</u>. They need <u>more time for fix</u> all of the fire hazards.
         C   D

6. **A:** Is Pam sick? I <u>noticed</u> <u>there was an ambulance</u> at her house.
                  A   B
           Correct: _____

   B: I <u>don't hope so</u>, but <u>I think she might be</u>.
          C   D

7. **A:** Did they <u>make you to stay</u> there all night?
                 A
           Correct: _____

   B: No, they didn't <u>make us stay</u> overnight, but <u>they didn't</u>
                   B   C

   <u>let us go</u> for hours.
     C

8. **A:** How did the police <u>convince him</u> <u>to talk</u>?
                     A   B
           Correct: _____

   B: <u>I guess so</u> <u>he was really tired</u>.
         C   D

NAME: _____   DATE: _____

UNIT 20 VOCABULARY EXERCISES

A   Complete the advertisement. Use the words in the box.

board	check your bags	ticket counter
carry-on bag	gate	tour guide
check in	~~take a tour~~	

Alaskan Animals by Air

Have you always wanted to see an Alaskan bear on a hike?
Well, that's not a good idea—it's dangerous! Instead,

_____take a tour_____ with *Alaskan Animals by Air*, and you'll
      1.

see animals from the plane! You can _____ our
                              2.

plane in the morning and relax all day. Our _____
                                     3.

will give you interesting information about the animals on the

ground.

The details:

Please visit our _____ on
              4.

Freeman Street. The plane takes off at 9 A.M.

from _____ 24 at the
      5.

airport. You must _____
            6.

at the gate. It is a small plane, so we can't

_____. And you may bring only
     7.

one _____.
      8.

B   **Complete the conversations. Use the words in the box.**

boarding pass	fasten our seatbelts	immigration officer
customs officers	hotel clerk	~~security officer~~

1. **A:** Excuse me. Can my grandchildren meet me at the gate?

   B: Ask that ____security officer____. He's next to the x-ray machine.

2. **A:** The _____ said our room will be ready at 2:00.

   B: OK. Let's come back later.

3. **A:** I'm going to use the restroom.

   B: That's not a good idea. The flight attendant told us to _____.

4. **A:** Do you think I can bring this fruit to Japan?

   B: No, I heard some _____ telling people that fruit is not

   allowed.

5. **A:** What did she say?

   B: She asked you to get out your _____. It's time to get on the

   plane.

6. **A:** Where were you?

   B: I was talking to the _____. He told me I can only stay in the

   United States for six months with this visa.

UNIT 20 GRAMMAR EXERCISES

Grammar to Communicate 1:
Reported Speech: Present Statements

A Read the sentences. Where does each person work? Write *A* (on an airplane), *C* (at airport customs), or *H* (at a hotel).

___A___ **1.** Lisa says to the passengers, "You must turn off all electronic devices."

_____ **2.** Pete says to the couple, "You must check out by 11:00 A.M."

_____ **3.** Pam says to the man, "I'm sorry, but your room won't be ready until 3:00."

_____ **4.** Roger says to the woman, "I need to know the reason for your visit."

_____ **5.** Paul says to the family, "I need you to fasten your seatbelts."

_____ **6.** Sara says to the man, "I'll have to check your bag. It won't fit under your seat."

_____ **7.** Dan says to the men, "There is a problem with your papers."

B Change the quoted speech in Exercise A to reported speech.

1. Lisa says (that) they must turn off all electronic devices. _____

2. _____

3. _____

4. _____

5. _____

6. _____

7. _____

NAME: _____   DATE: _____

Grammar to Communicate 2:
Reported Speech: Commands

A **Match the beginnings of the sentences with the endings. Write the correct letters.**

  _c_ **1.** The pilot told the passengers   **a.** to book the hotel.

  ____ **2.** The travel agent told his customer   **b.** to enjoy their meal.

  ____ **3.** The hotel manager told the employees **c.** ~~to enjoy the flight.~~

  ____ **4.** The guide on the bus tour told us   **d.** not to be late.

  ____ **5.** The waitress told the customers   **e.** to open her bag.

  ____ **6.** The security officer told the woman **f.** not to forget our cameras.

B **Read what happened to the Coyne boys on their family vacation. Write the exact words that people said to them.**

1. The security officer told us not to run in the airport.

The security officer told us, "Don't run in the airport."

2. The flight attendant told us to stay in our seats.

_____

3. Our mom told us not to bother the other passengers

_____

4. The hotel manager told us not to play on the grass.

_____

5. The guests at the pool told us to be quiet.

_____

6. The tour guide told us not to touch anything in the museum.

_____

7. The waiter told us not to make a mess.

_____

8. We told our parents to leave us at home the next time!

_____

Grammar to Communicate 3:
Reported Speech: Requests

A   Read each question. Circle the correct answer.

1. What did the flight attendant ask the passenger to do?
   She asked him to put his bag under **her seat** / (**his seat**).

2. What did the security officer ask you to do?
   She asked me to open **my bag** / **her bag**.

3. What did the cab driver ask the passengers to do?
   She asked them / **They asked her** to close their windows.

4. What did the hotel clerk ask the guests to do?
   She asked **her to give them** / **them to give her** their reservation number.

5. What did the passengers ask the flight attendant to do?
   They asked him / **He asked them** to give them some blankets.

B   Change the quoted requests to reported requests. Use the words in the box.

bus driver	flight attendant	passenger
cab driver	~~hotel clerk~~	travel agent

1. He asked, "Can you move me to another room?"
   He asked _the hotel clerk to move him to another room_.

2. She asked, "Can you find me a cheap hotel near the beach?"
   She asked _____.

3. She asked, "Could you show me your identification and boarding pass, sir?"
   She asked _____.

4. He asked, "Would you please take me to the airport?"
   He asked _____.

5. They asked "Could you give us some water, please?"
   They asked _____.

6. She asked, "Can you let me out at the next stop?"
   She asked _____.

Review and Challenge

Complete the conversation. Use the words in the box. (Be careful! There are extra words.)

ask	don't	not	to stay	wait
to ask	him	stay	to tell	~~we~~
asked	me	to	us	you

Tour guide: Please remember that you need to turn off your cell phones before you enter the museum.

Mr. Tam: What's he saying?

Mr. Tam's son: He says that _____we_____ need to turn off our cell phones.
1.

Tour guide: And please stay together when we get inside the museum.

Mr. Tam: What's that?

Mr. Tam's son: He told us _____ together inside the museum. Dad, can you
2.

_____ here a minute? I need to get my camera.
3.

Mr. Tam: Huh? What's that?

Mr. Tam's son: I _____ you to wait here a minute. My camera's in the bus.
4.

Mr. Tam: OK.

Mr. Tam's son: And please _____ the guide to wait for me.
5.

Mr. Tam: To what?

Mr. Tam's son: Ask _____ to wait for _____ to come back.
6.   7.

Mr. Tam: OK.

Tour guide: OK, so let's go inside. But please _____ enter the exhibit until
8.

the whole group is together.

Mr. Tam: Excuse me? What did he say? My hearing's not very good.

Man on the tour: He told _____ to go inside, but _____ to enter the exhibit
9.   10.

until the whole group is together.

Mr. Tam: Excuse me. My son told me _____ ask _____ to wait for
11.   12.

him. He left his camera on the bus.

Unit 1, page 1, vocabulary

A
2. wavy hair
3. straight hair
4. curly hair
5. mustaches
6. a beard

B
2. am going out with
3. a nice personality
4. sense of humor
5. get along with
6. a bad temper

Unit 1, page 3, grammar

Grammar to Communicate 1

A

Answers will vary depending on the student's and teacher's appearance.
2. I've got / I haven't got
3. I've got / I haven't got
4. I've got / I haven't got
5. My teacher's got / My teacher hasn't got
6. My teacher's got / My teacher hasn't got
7. My teacher's got / My teacher hasn't got
8. My teacher's got / My teacher hasn't got

B
2. b   3. b   4. b   5. a   6. a

Grammar To Communicate 2

A
2. No, I'm not
3. Yes, she is
4. No, he's not
5. Yes, they are
6. No, I'm not

B
2. am / 'm meeting
3. are / 're going
4. are / 're getting
5. am / 'm not spending
6. is getting
7. isn't having
8. is / 's studying

Grammar to Communicate 3

A
2. is having
3. aren't getting along
4. doesn't have
5. loves
6. isn't doing

B
1. isn't doing
2. Is she visiting; spends
3. get; has
4. Are your neighbors having; have

Review and Challenge
2. D: He's **studying** really hard.
3. C: Yes, and she **has** got a great sense of humor.
4. D: She's **got** a bad temper.
5. C: He **is** tall, and he has beautiful brown eyes.
6. C: No, but we **are getting** to know them.
7. C: No, they **aren't**, but they're still good friends.
8. A: Why **are you** wearing jeans?
9. D: They **are / 're staying** at a hotel.
10. D: I haven't got a pencil, but **I have / 've got** a pen.

Unit 2, page 7, vocabulary

A
2. a tourist
3. a farm
4. traffic
5. a parking space
6. public transportation

B
2. a factory
3. A field
4. pollution
5. parking
6. sunshine

Unit 2, page 8, grammar

Grammar to Communicate 1

A
2. are
3. small city
4. few
5. very little

B
2. There isn't much parking.
3. There are some parking spaces out back.
4. There isn't any public transportation.
5. There are very few fields.
6. There is very little traffic.
7. There are a lot of criminals.
8. There are no jobs.

Grammar to Communicate 2

A
2. b   4. f   6. c
3. a   5. e

B
2. There isn't enough
3. There are too many
4. There is / 's too much
5. There is / 's plenty of
6. There aren't enough

Answer Key

Grammar to Communicate 3

A

3. ✓
4. ✗, Both of the neighborhoods **are** friendly.
5. ✗, There isn't much parking in **either** neighborhood.
6. ✗, But parking is not a problem because **neither** of us has a car.
7. ✓
8. ✗, Both of the neighborhoods **are** large. OR **Neither** of the neighborhoods **is** large.

B

2. Both (of the) apartments are
3. either of the apartments / either apartment
4. Both (of the) apartments are
5. in both (of the) buildings
6. Neither of the buildings is / Neither building is
7. either of the landlords / either landlord

Review and Challenge

Dear Julia,

How are you? I think about you several times a day, but I never seem to have **enough** time to write. Anyway, I have **a few** minutes now, and I have a lot **of** news!

The new apartment is great. There are several **windows** in every room, so there's plenty **of** light. Actually, there's too much light right now—I have no curtains, and no time to buy any. The apartment's also very quiet. There are only three apartments in this building, and neither of my neighbors is home very much. There's only a little traffic on the street during the day, and **no** traffic at night.

What else? My neighbors seem friendly. Both **of** them are college students too. When I have a little free time, I'm going to invite them over for coffee. I'm really busy, but I'm lonely too. Anyway, I have **a lot of** homework, so I'll say good-bye for now. I'll write again soon.

Unit 3, page 12, vocabulary

A

2. missed	4. court	6. goal
3. runs	5. pass	

B

2. cheered	4. scored	6. points
3. lost to	5. was tied	

Unit 3, page 13, grammar

Grammar to Communicate 1

A

3. didn't score	5. beat	7. won
4. weren't	6. passed	8. didn't play

B

2. We didn't beat the best team. / The best team beat us.
3. We weren't relaxed before the game.
4. The game started late.
5. Our best player wasn't in good shape.
6. We expected to lose.
7. But we didn't feel good after the game.

Grammar to Communicate 2

A

3. Yes, it was. We almost won.
4. Yes, I did. I scored ten points.
5. No, I didn't. I went home.

B

3. Who was the best player on the team?
4. How many players were on the team?
5. Where did you play most of your games?
6. Why did you miss so many games?
7. What happened at the last game?
8. Who did the manager hire to be the new coach?

Grammar to Communicate 3

A

2. a   3. b   4. a   5. a   6. a

B

2. After the coach saw Jessica play, he invited her to join the team. OR
   The coach invited Jessica to join the team after he saw her play.
3. He wanted her on the team because she was an excellent player. OR
   Because she was an excellent player, he wanted her on the team.
4. Before Jessica joined the team, they / the team didn't win very often. OR
   They / The team didn't win very often before Jessica joined the team.
5. As soon as / After Jessica started playing, the team started to win. OR
   The team started to win as soon as / after Jessica started playing.
6. They / The team won the championship because Jessica was on the team. OR
   Because Jessica was on the team, they / the team won the championship.

7. After they won the championship, they went out to celebrate. OR
   They went out to celebrate after they won the championship.

Review and Challenge

2. A: **Did you** hear the news about Ben?
3. C: He **left** because he hurt his knee.
4. B: What **was the score** in last night's game?
5. D: I was late, so I **didn't get** a seat.
6. B: **As soon as** Raven left, they started to lose.
7. D: It was before he **started** school.
8. B: Who **won** the World Cup last year?
9. B: We lost because we **didn't have** our best player.

Unit 4, page 17, vocabulary

A

2. fell off the ladder
3. dropped
4. daydreaming
5. cut
6. fell down the stairs
7. went down the stairs
8. burning

B

2. iron   3. slip   4. chop

Unit 4, page 18, grammar

Grammar to Communicate 1

A

2. e   4. a   6. b
3. f   5. g   7. c

B

2. wasn't playing   5. wasn't walking
3. were sleeping   6. were talking
4. were walking   7. wasn't working; was driving

Grammar to Communicate 2

A

2. c   4. a   6. g
3. d   5. e   7. f

B

2. Who was driving?
3. Why were you driving?
4. Where was your mother sitting?
5. Were you and your mother wearing seatbelts?
6. How fast were you driving?
7. Was it raining a lot?

Grammar to Communicate 3

A

2. was working   5. took
3. cut   6. broke
4. wasn't paying   7. was raining

B

2. was going; fell
3. broke; dropped
4. burned; was ironing
5. slipped; was daydreaming
6. was chopping; cut

Review and Challenge

I had a terrible day last Friday. First, I didn't hear my alarm clock, so I **got** up late. I didn't have time to take a shower or eat my breakfast. I just got dressed and **ran** out the door. While I **was** walking to the train station, it started to rain. I didn't have an umbrella. I **didn't** want to get wet, so I started to run. I **was** running when I slipped and dropped my books. While I **was picking** them up, I heard the train. I ran to the station, but it was too late. The train was **leaving** when I got there. When I finally got to class, all of the students **were** leaving. Class was over! I walked back to the train station in the rain. Then I **went** home and got back into bed. I didn't **wake** up until the next morning.

Unit 5, page 22, vocabulary

A

2. change a diaper   4. dress
3. feed   5. give . . . a bath

B

2. get dressed up   4. throw away
3. wears casual clothes   5. repairs

Unit 5, page 23, grammar

Grammar to Communicate 1

A

2. a   4. a   6. a
3. b   5. b   7. b

B

3. used to get dressed up
4. used to repair
5. didn't use to give birth
6. used to make their own clothes

Answer Key

Grammar to Communicate 2

A

3. they did   6. they didn't
4. they didn't   7. they did
5. they didn't

B

2. Did people / women use to cook every day?
3. Did children use to obey their parents?
4. Did men use to do housework?
5. Did women / people use to live alone?
6. Did people / children use to go to bed early?

Grammar to Communicate 3

A

2. e   3. a   4. b   5. c   6. d

B

2. What did you use to do for fun?
3. How did you use to get to school?
4. Where did you use to work?
5. How much did you use to make?
6. How much did an apartment (downtown) use to cost?
7. How often did you use to eat out? OR Where did you use to eat out? OR When did you use to eat out?

Review and Challenge

2. B: We didn't **use to** have a car.
3. A: When **did women use to** get married?
4. B: How **did people use to** heat their homes?
5. B: Who **used to** cook in your house?
6. C: Did you **use to go** and watch her games?
7. C: No, she **didn't**.
8. C: I didn't use to like my mother, but now **I do**.
9. B: We didn't **use to argue** at all.

Unit 6, page 27, vocabulary

A

2. answer the door   5. am free
3. try out for   6. answer the phone
4. get . . . to go

B

2. g   4. c   6. f
3. a   5. b   7. e

Unit 6, page 29, grammar

Grammar to Communicate 1

A

2. D   4. P   6. P
3. P   5. D   7. D

B

2. 'll give   4. won't tell   6. won't hurt
3. 'll get   5. 'll help   7. won't be

Grammar to Communicate 2

A

2. I'll   4. isn't going to   6. I'll
3. are going to   5. We won't

B

2. is / 's going to feed   5. is / 's going to show
3. is going to come   6. will / 'll see
4. won't bother

Grammar to Communicate 3

A

3. is playing   6. is getting
4. isn't picking; is having   7. are coming
5. is attending

B

2. is / 's Melissa seeing
3. Is Bert playing
4. is / 's Bert doing
5. is / 's cutting
6. Are Bert's parents visiting

Review and Challenge

2. a   5. b   8. a
3. b   6. b   9. b
4. b   7. a   10. a

Unit 7, page 33, vocabulary

A

2. gets good grades   5. major in
3. gets a scholarship   6. take an exam
4. apply for

B

2. failed the class   5. takes the finals
3. pass the class   6. cheat
4. improve

Unit 7, page 34, grammar

Grammar to Communicate 1

A

2. a   4. b   6. a
3. a   5. c   7. c

B

3. ✗, if you cheat
4. ✓

5. ✗, If I don't do well

6. ✗, I will / 'll give you an F OR I am / 'm going to give you an F

7. ✗, if you don't get a scholarship

Grammar to Communicate 2

A

2. 2, 1   4. 2, 1   6. 1, 2
3. 2, 1   5. 1, 2   7. 2, 1

B

2. am / 'm going to register (will register)
3. am / 'm going to take (will take)
4. finishes
5. graduates
6. am / 'm going to apply (will apply)
7. am / 'm going to study (will study)
8. choose

Grammar to Communicate 3

A

2. might not   5. will
3. are not going to   6. may
4. will   7. will

B

2. may not get (might not get)
3. might work (may work)
4. will give
5. might do (may do)
6. will / 'll ask
7. are going to see
8. will / 'll pick

Review and Challenge

2. D: Your teacher **might not** like that.
3. A: I'm not **going to leave** until he calls.
4. D: Well, perhaps we'll be lucky and it **won't rain**.
5. D: But if we don't give him a chance, we **will / 'll never know**.
6. A: He **may / might transfer** next year.
7. A: If your work **doesn't improve**, you're going to fail.
8. B: You might **not get** the scholarship.
9. A: **As soon as** (When / After) we finish our exams, we're going to take a vacation.
10. D: We'll decide **as soon as we look** at all of the applications.

Unit 8, page 38, vocabulary

A

2. train   5. search
3. the day shift   6. the night shift
4. contact   7. overtime

B

2. quit   4. fired   6. heard from
3. handled   5. hired

Unit 8, page 40, grammar

Grammar to Communicate 1

A

2. hasn't   4. has   6. have
3. have   5. haven't   7. hasn't

B

2. She hasn't posted her résumé online.
3. She has / 's looked in the Sunday newspaper.
4. She hasn't contacted an employment agency.
5. She has / 's talked to the job counselor at school.
6. She has / 's registered for a computer course.

Grammar to Communicate 2

A

2. searching for a job   5. searching for a job
3. searching for a worker   6. searching for a job
4. searching for a worker   7. searching for a worker

B

2. hasn't gotten   5. haven't seen
3. has taken   6. has / 's found
4. have / 've given

Grammar to Communicate 3

A

2. c   4. e   6. d
3. a   5. g   7. f

B

2. Have you ever applied for a job here?
3. Have they ever fired an employee?
4. Has she finished the training program?
5. Have you ever owned your own business?
6. Have you ever handled large amounts of money?
7. Has he ever used a cash register?

Review and Challenge

2. haven't   5. had   8. has
3. hasn't   6. yet   9. you've
4. he's   7. never   10. ever

Answer Key

A

2. widow
3. honeymoon
4. fights
5. argued

B

2. marriage
3. widower
4. birth
5. newlyweds

Unit 9, page 45, grammar

Grammar to Communicate 1

A

2. since   3. for   4. since   5. for

B

2. a. since last year / since the separation
   b. for a year
3. a. since February
   b. for eight months
4. a. since kindergarten
   b. for many years
5. a. since May
   b. for five months

Grammar to Communicate 2

A

2. have / 've been living alone for
3. hasn't been getting along; since
4. hasn't been spending; since
5. has been waiting for
6. has been staying; since

B

3. ✗, for a month
4. ✗, They have known each other
5. ✓
6. ✓
7. ✗, She has not / hasn't been sleeping

Grammar to Communicate 3

A

2. e   3. b   4. a   5. c

B

2. How long have you been looking for a roommate?
3. Have you been getting a lot of calls?
4. Have your other roommates been helping you?
5. How long has the landlord been renting this apartment?
6. Has the landlord been working on the place recently?

Review and Challenge

Rachel: Betsy, what's wrong? You look terrible.
Betsy: Lately Danny and I haven't been getting along.
Rachel: I'm sorry to hear that. How long have you **been** having problems?
Betsy: **For** a few months. But it **has** been getting a lot worse recently.
Rachel: What do you mean?
Betsy: Well, Danny's been **staying** out late almost every night. He **hasn't** been spending any time with me or the kids lately.
Rachel: What do you mean? **Has he** been working late?
Betsy: He says that he has, but I don't believe him.
Rachel: Why not?
Betsy: I don't know. It's just a feeling.
Rachel: How long **have** you and Danny **been** married?
Betsy: For 15 years. We'**ve been** together since high school.
Rachel: And has he ever **lied** to you?
Betsy: No, he **has** never lied to me. (OR hasn't **ever**)
Rachel: Then why don't you believe him now?
Betsy: Hmm . . . Maybe you have a point.

Unit 10, page 49, vocabulary

A

2. successful
3. clear
4. calm
5. attractive
6. fashionable

B

2. secret
3. strange
4. romantic
5. awful
6. star

Unit 10, page 51, grammar

Grammar to Communicate 1

A

2. bad, badly
3. attractive, attractively
4. neat, neatly
5. fast, fast
6. hard, hard
7. slow, slowly

B

2. She acts badly.
3. Movie stars dress attractively.
4. Television chefs usually cook neatly.
5. On police shows, the officers drive fast.
6. The director works hard.
7. That actor learns slowly.

Grammar to Communicate 2

A

2. They live dangerously.
3. He is / 's behaving politely.
4. They are / 're talking romantically.
5. She speaks softly.
6. You drive nervously.
7. She dresses fashionably.

B

2. awful 4. clearly 6. successful
3. softly 5. terrific 7. angry

Grammar to Communicate 3

A

2. pretty 4. pretty 6. pretty
3. really 5. very 7. very

B

3. ✗, pretty terrible
4. ✗, really perfectly
5. ✗, really awful
6. ✓
7. ✗, extremely / really quickly

Review and Challenge

2. B: Good talk show hosts interview **interesting people** and ask really excellent questions.
3. B: Really **popular** television shows sometimes continue for a very long time.
4. A: That show was **really** awful, and the tickets were extremely expensive!
5. D: Chef Rick's cakes always look beautiful, but they taste pretty **terrible**.
6. A: I can't **hear well** because they are speaking very softly.
7. C: It's never **slow** or boring.
8. B: Everyone was laughing really **hard**.
9. A: Please be **quiet**.

Unit 11, page 55, vocabulary

A

2. elephant 4. dolphins
3. chimpanzees 5. rabbits

B

2. f 4. a 6. b
3. e 5. c 7. d

Unit 11, page 57, grammar

Grammar to Communicate 1

A

2. better than 5. farther than
3. heavier than 6. smaller than
4. more quietly than

B

2. Rats have the shortest lives.
3. Donkeys are the most stubborn.
4. Whales swim the most quickly.
5. Chimps can be trained the most easily.
6. Whales are the heaviest.

Grammar to Communicate 2

A

3. the most time 6. fewer visitors than
4. the least time 7. the fewest hours
5. less noise than

B

2. Chobe has more elephants than Kruger.
3. Chobe has less space than Kruger.
4. Addo has the least space of the three.
5. Chobe has fewer visitors than Addo.
6. Kruger has the most visitors of the three.
7. Kruger has fewer elephants than Chobe.

Grammar to Communicate 3

A

2. a 4. a 6. a
3. a 5. b

B

2. My cat can't walk as far as my dog (can).
3. My cat didn't cost as much as my parrot (did).
4. I don't sing as well as my parrot (does).
5. I don't need as much sleep as my cat (does).
6. My dogs aren't as cute as my cat (is).

Review and Challenge

2. B: Dogs need as **much** love as children.
3. A: Gorillas are heavier and taller than chimps. (Delete **more**.)
4. D: A dog isn't as intelligent **as** a gorilla is.
5. C: Elephants are the **biggest** land animals.
6. C: Cats don't learn as **easily** as dogs.
7. B: There are **fewer** dogs in my country than in the United States.
8. B: Dolphins can swim more **quickly** than people can.

Answer Key

9. A: The zoo had **fewer** visitors last year than the year before.
10. C: Snails move the **most slowly** of all animals.

Unit 12, page 61, vocabulary

A

2. seating
3. specials
4. enjoying herself
5. salad bar
6. serving
7. treating

B

2. dessert
3. appetizers
4. help themselves
5. stuff themselves
6. napkins

Unit 12, page 63, grammar

Grammar to Communicate 1

A

1. you
2. myself; you
3. me; yourself
4. himself; himself
5. her; yourselves
6. them; themselves

B

3. ✓
4. ✗, yourselves
5. ✓
6. ✗, herself
7. ✗, each other
8. ✗, me

Grammar to Communicate 2

A

2. a
3. a
4. a
5. b
6. b
7. a

B

2. b
3. a
4. c
5. d
6. e
7. h
8. g

Grammar to Communicate 3

A

2. One, The other
3. The others
4. The other
5. Another
6. The other

B

2 One is lemon, another is chocolate, and the other is strawberry.
9 I don't care. Surprise me!
1 What kind of cakes are those?
8 Which one? The chocolate or the strawberry?
4 Well, I like the lemon, but the others are good too.
5 OK. I'll have two slices of the lemon. One for here and another to go.
3 They all sound delicious. Which one do you recommend?

7 So give me one of the others.
6 I'm sorry, but there's only one slice of that one.

Review and Challenge

2. each other
3. yourselves
4. themselves
5. himself
6. other
7. another
8. one
9. the one
10. myself

Unit 13, page 67, vocabulary

A

2. downloaded
3. burned CDs
4. camcorder
5. installed
6. Web

B

2. remote control
3. online
4. operate
5. software
6. charge

Unit 13, page 68, grammar

Grammar to Communicate 1

A

2. We can install any software.
3. He isn't (He's not) able to operate the remote control.
4. These days, people are able to make movies at home.
5. I'm able to send e-mail, but I can't open my messages.
6. I'm sorry, but we aren't (we're not) able to fix your DVD player.

B

2. haven't been able to access; can help
3. can play; can't burn
4. has been able to operate; can do
5. can do; can't be

Grammar to Communicate 2

A

2. My great grandfather was able to fix any car.
3. We couldn't charge the battery.
4. I couldn't find the website.
5. You were able to use a computer at 5 years old.
6. Before airplanes, most people couldn't travel long distances.

B

2. weren't able to access
3. was able to record
4. weren't able to burn
5. were able to fix

6. wasn't able to install
7. were able to communicate

Grammar to Communicate 3

A

2. can have babies; will be able to have babies
3. can use a computer; will be able to use a computer
4. can walk on the moon; will be able to walk on Mars
5. can help people live longer; will be able to help people live forever
6. can travel to the moon; will be able to live on the moon

B

2. Will they be able to order
3. Will I be able to use
4. Will I be able to use
5. Will they be able to access
6. will they be able to access

Review and Challenge

Dear Doctor Al,

Until last year, I **was** able to work on the computer for ten hours a day with no problem. Lately, however, I've been getting terrible headaches, and I have not been able to work for more than an hour. Last week, I **was** not able to finish an important project because I couldn't use the computer. My boss is angry. I think I might lose my job. And if I am not able to use a computer, I will never **be** able to find another job. So far, no one **has been** able to help me. You are my last hope. Please help!

Sincerely,

Sick of the computer

Dear Sick of the Computer,

I'm surprised that your doctor **wasn't able to help** (OR **couldn't help**) you. Your problem is very common, and there are many things that you **can do**. First of all, go to my website and you will find links to some excellent eye doctors. Any one of them will be able to help you. But here are some things you can do by yourself.

Make sure that you **are** able to look straight at the middle of your computer screen without moving your head up or down. If you need to move your head, change the position of your chair or your computer. And when you are working on the computer, take a short break every 15 minutes. If you **can't** get up and move around, just look away from the computer screen. If you do these two simple things, I think your headaches will go away.

Good luck!

Doctor Al

Unit 14, page 72, vocabulary

A

2. take out the trash
3. hold
4. apologize
5. obey

B

2. punishes
3. strict
4. crosses
5. bothers

Unit 14, page 73, grammar

Grammar to Communicate 1

A

2. No. He has to / 's got to / must take out the trash.
3. No. She has to / 's got to / must do the dishes.
4. No. They have to / 've got to / must turn off the TV.
5. No. They have to / have got to / must behave well.
6. No. They have to / have got to / must obey their mother.

B

2. Does your little boy have to do any chores?
3. Do I have to obey her?
4. Do I have to finish my vegetables?
5. Do the kids have to go to school today?
6. Does your daughter have to take classes this summer?

Grammar to Communicate 2

A

2. f   4. a   6. d
3. b   5. e

B

2. mustn't
3. mustn't
4. doesn't have to
5. mustn't
6. don't have to
7. don't have to

Grammar to Communicate 3

A

2. had to put
3. didn't have to share
4. had to babysit
5. didn't have to do
6. had to study
7. didn't have to take care of

B

2. did you have to walk
3. did your parents have to pay
4. did the students have to clean
5. did you have to go
6. did you have to share

Answer Key

Review and Challenge

2. D: Of course you **do**!
3. C: He **doesn't have to** pay anything.
4. D: No, but you must **stay** next to me.
5. A: Why does he **have** to come with us?
6. C: I **had to** babysit for my little sister.
7. A: The kids **didn't have** to go to school because of the snow.
8. D: My son's sick, so I had to **take** the day off.
9. A: In my culture, children **must not / mustn't** talk during meals.
10. A: **Did you have** to go to school yesterday?

Unit 15, page 77, vocabulary

2. puts her elbows
3. interrupts
4. talk about people behind their backs
5. cover her mouth
6. licks
7. talks with her mouth full
8. whisper

Unit 15, page 78, grammar

Grammar to Communicate 1

A

2. should   4. shouldn't   6. shouldn't
3. shouldn't   5. shouldn't

B

2. should I sit?   4. should I talk to?
3. should I put my hands?   5. should I take?

Grammar to Communicate 2

A

2. should be whispering
3. should be using a napkin
4. should be carrying
5. should be listening
6. should be working

B

2. She should be eating her vegetables. She shouldn't be feeding them to the dog.
3. You shouldn't be drinking milk from the carton. You should be using a glass.
4. She should be serving her guests. She shouldn't be serving herself.
5. They shouldn't be getting on the bus. They should be waiting for others to get off first.

Grammar to Communicate 3

A

2. a   4. c   6. b
3. c   5. a   7. c

B

2. should; have to
3. have to; don't have to
4. don't have to; shouldn't
5. have to; have to
6. don't have to; shouldn't

Review and Challenge

Ray: What are you doing here in the kitchen? You should be **spending** time with your guests.

Shana: But I have to cook.

Ray: Well, the guests look very uncomfortable.

Shana: Well, what **should** I do? Someone **has** to finish cooking the dinner.

Ray: You should go out there and talk to your guests. And you **shouldn't** leave them alone again. I'll finish in here.

Shana: Thanks, but you **don't** have to do that. You're busy, and they're my guests.

Ray: You're right. I **don't have** to help you. But I want to.

Shana: But you should **be** studying for your exams.

Ray: I've finished studying. Now tell me, what **do** I have to do?

Shana: Well, the meat has to cook for 30 minutes, but you have to turn it over after 20 minutes. It has to cook on both sides.

Ray: That's it?

Shana: Yes. Everything else is ready.

Unit 16, page 82, vocabulary

A

2. slamming the door   3. driveway   4. garden

B

2. gardeners   5. musician
3. junk   6. chat
4. shouting

Unit 16, page 84, grammar

Grammar to Communicate 1

A

2. a   4. b   6. a
3. b   5. a

B
2. They must have good jobs.
3. They must have a gardener.
4. They must be old.
5. They must be retired.
6. They must live far away.

Grammar to Communicate 2

A
2. d   4. b   6. e
3. a   5. g   7. c

B
2. must be dating   5. must be working
3. must be babysitting   6. must be practicing
4. must be moving   7. must be walking

Grammar to Communicate 3

A
3. ✓   4. ✓   5. ✗, in a bad mood

B
2. can't   4. must not / mustn't
3. can't   5. must not / mustn't

Review and Challenge

Mary: I can't wait to hear about the Cohen's trip! I think I'll go over there.
Steve: I don't think that's a good idea. They got in really late last night. They **must** be sleeping.
Mary: Are you kidding? They can't be **sleeping**! It's 11:00. They always get up early.
Steve: Yeah, but they didn't get home until 3:00 A.M. They **must** be tired.
Mary: Well one of them must **be** awake. I can see lights over there. I'm going over.
Mary: Yoo hoo, Sal? Ethel? Are you there?
Sal: Mary! Is that you?
Mary: Yes. Welcome home! How was your trip? You must **have** a million photos. Where's Ethel?
Sal: She's sleeping.
Mary: Oh, I'm so sorry.
Sal: That's OK. Come on in. But I don't have any photos to show you.
Mary: Oh come on! You **can't** be serious. You always take photos.
Sal: Well, not this time. I didn't even take my camera.
Mary: You must be **joking**.
Sal: You're right, I am joking. You know me too well, Mary. Anyway, have a seat and I'll make us some coffee. Then I'll show you the pictures.

Unit 17, page 88, vocabulary

A
2. common   4. get in shape
3. vitamin C   5. high cholesterol

B
2. weak   4. blood pressure
3. calcium   5. have surgery

Unit 17, page 89, grammar

Grammar to Communicate 1

A
2. It is / 's necessary for toddlers to take a nap every day.
3. It isn't / 's not normal for teenagers to sleep all day.
4. It is / 's normal for infants to sleep most of the day.
5. It is / 's common for middle-aged people to gain weight.
6. It is / 's a good idea for children over three to visit the dentist twice a year.

B
3. for pregnant women to get morning sickness
4. for healthy adults to have a cholesterol test every five years
5. to have a lot of pain after this kind of surgery
6. to exercise every day
7. for you to lose weight

Grammar to Communicate 2

A
2. f   4. e   6. d
3. a   5. b   7. g

B
2. too cold; warm enough   5. too high
3. too thin   6. old enough
4. very hot   7. very busy

Grammar to Communicate 3

A
2. to see better
3. to get a cleaning
4. to buy some cold medicine
5. to get in shape
6. to prevent a cold
7. to stop a headache

B
2. She's studying to be a doctor to help people.
3. I'm on a diet to lose weight.
4. He washes his hands several times a day to stay healthy.

Answer Key

5. He is having knee surgery to be able to run.
6. I put a bandage on the cut to keep it clean.
7. She is resting a lot to get stronger.

Review and Challenge

2. B: It's not a good idea **for him** to travel right now.
3. B: It's **very quiet**, so it's easy to relax.
4. C: It will be impossible **to** operate if he's too weak.
5. C: She isn't able to take care of herself anymore, and we are **too busy** to help her.
6. C: You aren't getting enough exercise to **lose weight**, and your cholesterol is too high.
7. A: He is **too sick** to have visitors.
8. D: I needed to come home **to rest**.
9. C: That medicine **isn't** strong enough.
10. B: It is necessary **for all employees** to know CPR.

Unit 18, page 93, vocabulary

A

2. prefers
3. is into
4. sewing
5. dislikes
6. am tired of

B

2. is good at
3. hike
4. knitting
5. consider
6. can't stand

Unit 18, page 95, grammar

Grammar to Communicate 1

A

2. Playing
3. Knitting
4. Taking
5. Camping
6. Spending
7. Being

B

2. Watching too much TV is bad for kids.
3. Riding a bike without a helmet is dangerous.
4. Taking care of a horse isn't cheap.
5. Swimming alone isn't a good idea.
6. Going to the mall is boring.

Grammar to Communicate 2

A

2. like going
3. of getting
4. into camping
5. to being
6. at playing
7. up knitting
8. on studying

B

2. Many children dream of becoming famous.
3. We are looking forward to going on vacation.
4. Please think about joining the team.
5. He's good at doing things with his hands.
6. They are concentrating on learning to cook.
7. We're excited about winning the game.

Grammar to Communicate 3

A

3. ✓
4. ✗, to win
5. ✓
6. ✓
7. ✗, dancing
8. ✗, fishing

B

2. They dislike baking.
3. I'm going to stop running.
4. We are learning to paint.
5. Do you want to dance?
6. She's considering taking guitar lessons.
7. Of course we hope to win.

Review and Challenge

2. seeing
3. having
4. swimming
5. to swim
6. to ask
7. losing
8. being
9. to have
10. to surprise

Unit 19, page 99, vocabulary

A

2. ambulance
3. paramedics
4. suspects
5. advised
6. fire hazards

B

2. notice
3. encouraged
4. guess
5. speeding
6. ticket

Unit 19, page 101, grammar

Grammar to Communicate 1

A

2. she
3. he
4. her
5. She
6. him
7. He
8. her
9. He
10. her
11. He
12. her

B

2. The fire inspector advised the landlord to fix the problem.
3. The firefighters ordered the tenants to leave the building.
4. Ana doesn't want the police officer to give her a ticket.

5. The paramedics convinced the old woman to go to the hospital.
6. The injured woman needs an ambulance to take her to the hospital.
7. She allowed the paramedics to help her.

Grammar to Communicate 2

A
2. Everyone thinks (that) there aren't enough police officers.
3. The police believe (that) they need the help of the people in the community.
4. The people in the neighborhood suspect (that) the police don't care about them.
5. The police don't believe (that) the neighborhood's people want to help them.
6. Everyone hopes (that) the neighborhood will be safe in the future.

B
2. guess so
3. think so
4. guess not
5. don't think so
6. don't believe so

Grammar to Communicate 3

A
2. didn't let
3. let
4. didn't make
5. made
6. made

B
2. didn't let them stay inside
3. didn't make me get out of the ambulance
4. didn't let them open
5. made him get out
6. let them take the elevator

Review and Challenge
2. C: He **told me (us)** to hire a lawyer.
3. D: No, I **don't think so.**
4. C: I think **that** she was scared.
5. D: They need **more time to fix** all of the fire hazards.
6. C: **I hope not**, but I think she might be.
7. A: Did they **make you stay** there all night?
8. C: **I guess** he was really tired.

A
2. board
3. tour guide
4. ticket counter
5. gate
6. check in
7. check your bags
8. carry-on bag

B
2. hotel clerk
3. fasten our seatbelts
4. customs officers
5. boarding pass
6. immigration officer

Grammar to Communicate 1

A
2. H
3. H
4. C
5. A
6. A
7. C

B
2. Pete says (that) they must check out by 11:00 A.M.
3. Pam says (that) she's sorry, but his room won't be ready until 3:00.
4. Roger says (that) he needs to know the reason for her visit.
5. Paul says (that) he needs them to fasten their seatbelts.
6. Sara says (that) she'll have to check his bag. It won't fit under his seat.
7. Dan says (that) there is a problem with their papers.

Grammar to Communicate 2

A
2. a   3. d   4. f   5. b   6. e

B
2. The flight attendant told us, "Stay in your seats."
3. Our mom told us, "Don't bother the other passengers."
4. The hotel manager told us, "Don't play on the grass."
5. The guests at the pool told us, "Be quiet."
6. The tour guide told us, "Don't touch anything in the museum."
7. The waiter told us, "Don't make a mess."
8. We told our parents, "Leave us at home the next time!"

Grammar to Communicate 3

A
2. my bag
3. She asked them
4. them to give her
5. They asked him

Answer Key

B

2. the travel agent to find her a cheap hotel near the beach
3. the passenger to show her his identification and boarding pass
4. the cab driver to take him to the airport
5. the flight attendant to give them some water
6. the bus driver to let her out at the next stop

Review and Challenge

2. to stay
3. wait
4. asked
5. ask
6. him
7. me
8. don't
9. us
10. not
11. to
12. you